THE HISTORY OF THE WORLD IN 12 SOCCER MATCHES

STEFANO BIZZOTTO

TRANSLATED BY WILL SCHUTT

MELVILLE HOUSE BROOKLYN • LONDON

History of the World in 12 Soccer Matches: Stefano Bizzotto;
translated by Will Schutt

First published in English 2026 by Melville House
Stefano Bizotto, Storia del Mundo en 12 partiti de calcio. Originally published in Italy by il Saggiatore.

This book was translated thanks to a grant awarded by the Italian Ministry of Foreign Affairs and International Cooperation.

First Melville House Printing: March 2026

Distributed by Penguin Random House LLC,
1745 Broadway, New York, NY 10019 USA
www.penguinrandomhouse.com

Melville House Publishing
46 John Street
Brooklyn, NY 11201
and
Melville House UK
Suite 2000
16/18 Woodford Road
London E7 0HA

mhpbooks.com
@melvillehouse

ISBN: 978-1-68589-229-6
ISBN: 978-1-68589-230-2 (eBook)

Library of Congress Control Number: 2025950074
Designed by Beste Doğan

Printed in the United States of America
10 9 8 7 6 5 4 3 2 1

A catalog record for this book is available from the Library of Congress

The authorized representative in the EU for product safety and compliance is Easy Access System Europe, Mustamäe tee 50, 10621 Tallinn, Estonia.
gpsr.requests@easproject.com

To my father
who loved history
and worshipped soccer

Photo Credits

Introduction: The History Emporium/Alamy Foto Stock
Chapter 1: Pictorial Press / Alamy Foto Stock
Chapter 2: The Smith Archive / Alamy Foto Stock
Chapter 8: Werner Otto / Alamy Foto Stock
Chapter 10: Gert Kilian/ullstein bild via Getty Images
Chapter 12: Franck Fife / afp via Getty Images
All other photos courtesy of il Saggiatore.

CONTENTS

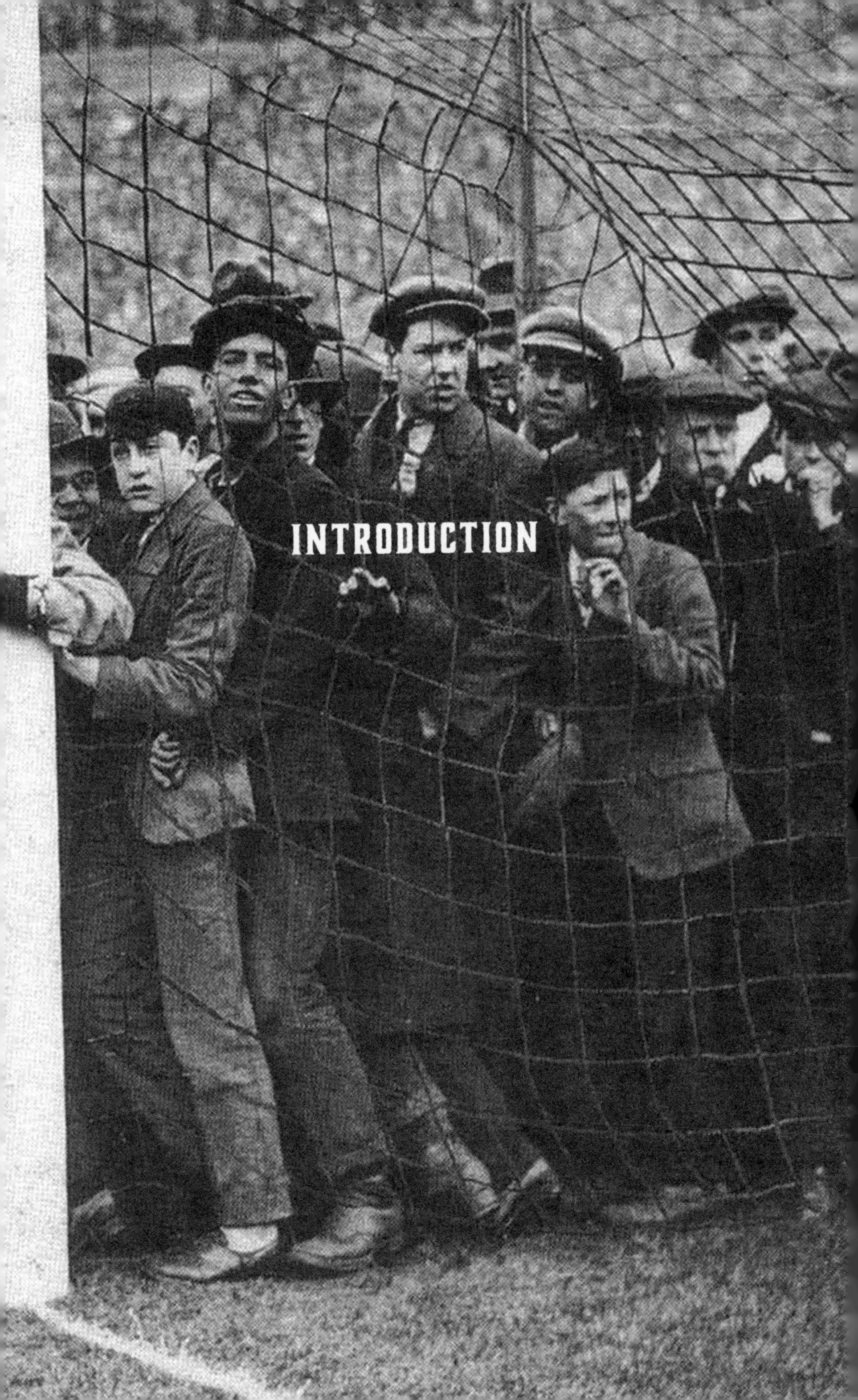

INTRODUCTION

THERE'S SOCCER AND then there's soccer. There are matches and then there are matches. Every match begins when the referee blows the whistle; many last just ninety minutes—or one hundred, given the trend of super-extended stoppage times these days—with no one having retained even the faintest memory of them. How did the match go? Who won? What was on the line? The questions hang in the air, awaiting a response that never comes.

But once in a while, even the least remarkable match intersects with capital *H* History and changes the fate of an individual or a community or a nation. The players on the field might not even know it. It doesn't take much: a shot off the post rather than into the net, a referee's whistle or failure to blow the whistle, a coach's call. That combined with what's going on in the background. A governing party, say, that morphs into a regime and exploits the world's most played sport for its own gain.

Soccer can trigger war, and it can also do the opposite and interrupt a conflict, even if just for a few hours or days. That was what happened at the height of the First World War.

The Christmas Truce of 1914 seems ripped from the pages of a novel, but reading eyewitness accounts of the event, you realize much of the story must be true.

That is precisely where this book begins: Christmas 1914. It's the start of a journey that will take us all the way to the present and touch on other wars, like that in the Balkans, which, according to one school of thought, has its origins in a soccer match. In between, other stories, not only war stories but tales of personal and collective drama, of murky deaths, and dreams smashed against the walls of state. Had it not been for a horse and its rider, Wembley Stadium, packed with 250,000 people, would have been the stage of a tragedy worse than the Heysel Stadium disaster. The one difference was what caused it: not, as in the 1980s, the murderous delirium of hooligans from across the Channel, but simply an incorrect head count on the part of those who organized the England Cup final a hundred years ago.

Every Sunday that I show up for work in Turin, I can't help but look up at the Basilica of Superga. And every time I think to myself, if only the pilot of the plane carrying the Grande Torino back from Portugal had flown the aircraft a hundred feet higher, the crash that brought an end to Italy's greatest ever team would never have happened. Or if Torino had lost to Inter Milan four days earlier, there never would have been an away game in Lisbon, and Superga would still be a place of worship like any other and not the mecca for thousands of Granata supporters and other soccer fans that it is now. And that marvelous team would have continued to inspire a country that had seen in it a symbol of redemption after the devastation of war. Hence the protagonist of our story becomes Inter Milan's Benito Lorenzi, who would forever regret not having capitalized on at least one of his openings to score.

Benito Lorenzi, Matthias Sindelar, Viktor Ponedelnik, Carlos Caszely, Lutz Eigendorf, Wim van Hanegem. These are some of the figures—perhaps not all well known to the general reader—who will accompany you through this century brimming with stories. Don't waste your time searching for a narrative thread from one chapter to the next. What follows are simply eleven stories—eleven plus one that crosses into the twenty-first century and touches on terrorism, ISIS, and Islamic jihad. Paris, November 13, 2015. That day also involved a soccer match between the French and German national teams. In the end, one is left with the feeling that soccer isn't just a sport where the object is to score one more goal than your opponent. Arrigo Sacchi called soccer "the most important of the least important things." He had a point.

CHAPTER 1

THE TRUCE:
THE DAY SOCCER STOPPED THE FIRST WORLD WAR

MATCH
Royal Saxon Regiment vs. Lancashire Fusiliers

FINAL SCORE
3–2

WHEN
December 25, 1914

WHERE
The Western Front, probably near Ypres

AS IF BY magic, the wind dies down. The rain stops falling. The sky is finally clear—so clear you feel compelled to count every star. It's cold, but the worst thing is the mud that seeps into your boots and sticks to your feet. There's more. When you move along the trench, or venture outside the trench and into what everyone calls no-man's-land, you're bound to stumble upon a grim sight: the rotting bodies of fellow soldiers, soldiers who've been dead for days, sometimes weeks. By now you hardly pay them any mind. The ice has covered up any trace of the mortal wounds on those poor boys' bodies.

This is war. You don't know how it started, and more importantly, you can't say how it will end. December 1914, the Western Front. A strip of land that runs from the Swiss Alps to the North Sea: thousands of miles, tens of thousands of soldiers. The Germans are the invading army; the Belgians and French defend their borders with the help of the English. Young men in their twenties, sometimes younger, had been told in September, "It'll all be over by Christmas at the latest, and you can go back home." Home for Christmas? Maybe, but which Christmas? Not this one, that's for sure. What began as a war of crossing enemy lines has quickly become a war of entrenchment. Neither party can gain real ground. Meanwhile, people are dying.

In 1914, "real" soccer was nearly half a century old—that is, the sport organized and codified with a rule book. The FA Cup, the first official soccer trophy, had been awarded since 1872. Later came the competitions between national teams, first between the representatives of the British federations and then everyone else.

The first match between Germany and England took place on Easter Monday, 1908. Or more accurately: a group of English amateurs was randomly assembled, herded onto a ferry, and then onto a train bound for Berlin. Yet they still managed to win 5–1 and teach their ill-equipped German counterparts how the game is played. The next year they did the same in Oxford, widening the gulf between the two contenders even further. Ten players came over from Germany. The eleventh, Willy Baumgärtner, awaited his teammates in

London, his adopted home. The match ended 9–0, and by all accounts the performance of the German goalkeeper Adolf Werner was fantastic. When the game ended, the English players themselves carried him on their shoulders and let him take the ball home, showing him the kind of treatment you'd expect for a center forward who'd scored a hat trick. Which is to say that, had there been a different goalkeeper, the match might have ended 15–nil.

It was just five years before the First World War but no one in Europe had the slightest inkling of the carnage to come. For one thing, the German emperor Wilhelm II was, at the time, an honorary colonel in the British Dragoons. And in 1914, when he attended Kiel Sailing Week, he was photographed wearing a British admiral's uniform. Soon after came the assassination in Sarajevo and a shifting network of alliances that found Germany and Britain on opposite sides. The 9–0 match in Berlin? Werner's awesome shot-stopping blocks? Who could remember? Indeed, who could have foreseen that many of the people involved in that match would be sent to fight and die in the war?

THE AREA WAS around Ypres, a town in the Flanders region of Belgium. For two years, a road cycling race had been held there—one that would become legendary. In the aftermath of the Second World War, Fiorenzo Magni would later earn the nickname Il Leone delle Fiandre—"the Lion of Flanders"—after winning the Tour three times in a row. But there were other lions: those poor men whose waking objective was to make it out alive. The luckiest would succeed; everyone else would take their last breath in Ypres.

By Christmas Eve, the numbers of the war dead were chilling: 160,000 British soldiers, 300,000 Germans, and as many Frenchmen—all killed in just a few weeks. There was no way to explain such carnage to those shipped out to die.

When the war was over, Winston Churchill said about Ypres, "A more sacred place for the British race does not exist in the world." By the end of the conflict, four battles were fought there, and the city reduced to rubble. In 1927, a monument was erected listing the names of twenty-five thousand British soldiers who had no burial because their bodies were missing or too badly damaged to identify.

In this climate, perhaps because Christmas was approaching, many were ready to say they'd had enough. Especially ground troops, who were beginning to realize that they had a lot more in common with the average soldier behind enemy lines than they did with their superior officers. But convincing generals to lay down their arms was out of the question; were peace to reign, too many generals would find themselves out of work. Besides, it was not as if everyone deep in the trenches agreed with the higher-ups. A real rift had opened in the German army. Prussian troops had no desire to make a deal with the enemy, though their Bavarian counterparts and Württemberg's troops were another story. It was a battle of hawks and doves, you might say.

A few weeks before Christmas, there had been a general

ceasefire. The Germans laid down their arms; the British did the same. But out from behind the "good" German troops popped the "bad" German troops, who opened fire. It was a bloodbath.

SUSPEND PLAY ON account of the war? That was out of the question. Or at least it was in England, where the Football League had begun its twenty-seventh season on September 1, 1914—on schedule. It was business as usual: twenty teams, thirty-eight days, matches home and away. Everyone had it out for Blackburn, the reigning champion. But because other athletic leagues had suspended play, the decision didn't pass without commentary. Newspapers published letters excoriating clubs, players, and fans alike. To many, soccer was draining human resources that would otherwise have gone toward fighting the German enemy. To readers' frontal attacks were added those from the world of politics and culture. Even someone as crazy about the sport as the author of *Sherlock Holmes*, Sir Arthur Conan Doyle, wrote, "There was a time for everything, but there is only time for one thing now, and that thing is war . . . If a footballer had strength of limb let them serve and march in the field of battle." Still, one way or another, they carried on with the season. But things were changing. Boys were dying on battlefields in droves; that could not be ignored.

Funds were raised and several football clubs lent out their pitches for military training. The turning point came with the formation of the Football Battalion, a group of professional players embedded in the 17th Service Battalion, Middlesex Regiment, as well as supporters who were attracted by the prospect of training alongside their favorite players. One of the first to join was Frank Buckley. Buckley wasn't just anybody. He played for Derby County, and in February 1914 had the honor of donning the national team jersey.

In no time, soccer balls began turning up on ferries crossing the English Channel. Senior officers knew that an occasional match could help boost morale. It was like a scene from half a century earlier, when ships departing English ports for Genoa, Barcelona, Marseilles, and Buenos Aires were filled not only with workers crossing the globe to build railways but also with soccer balls so they could carry on their favorite pastime. Only now the situation was entirely different.

THERE WAS SOMETHING unnatural, almost miraculous, about the silence, especially after the grim soundtrack of those weeks: days filled with the deafening noise of machine guns, with the blasts of land mines exacting their heavy death toll, the excruciating screams of those about to take their last breath. Just silence, from one trench to another.

Suddenly from the German side came the first notes of a song: "Stille Nacht, heilige Nacht." *Silent Night*. Were they not at war, it would be the most natural thing in the world. It was only a few hours before Christmas, and that song, which everyone in Germany knew by heart, is a hymn to the birth of Jesus. Then something else. British lookouts spotted small lights emanating from the enemy trench. What appeared to be the signs of a nighttime attack turned out to be candles that the soldiers had placed on saplings to celebrate the holiday. "Good old Fritz!" shouted His Majesty's subjects. And the Germans floated an idea: "We don't shoot, you don't shoot." After a moment's hesitation, their proposal was accepted. The protagonists didn't know it, but they were about to write a page of history.

There would be a ceasefire, and that ceasefire would come from the bottom ranks. Neither side's generals knew anything about it; it was the doing of those poor souls sent to the front lines of a dirty war. And therefore no one dared tell their superiors; severe punishments would surely have been handed down. Instead, a miracle happened. The guns fell silent, thanks to those astonishing boys from Munich and Manchester, Hamburg and Liverpool. Benedict XV had tried to do it before them, but to no avail. The pope's appeal for a Christmas ceasefire ("that the guns may fall silent at least upon the night the angels sang") had fallen on deaf ears.

In some parts along the Western Front, no-man's-land was no more than a few dozen meters wide. It was easy to shout across the trenches. And because so many German boys had a smattering of English, they began to converse. Just a few words: "Happy Christmas," "Frohe Weihnachten." Words that well up from the heart. Then sleep came over them. Tomorrow would be a special day.

IN 1914, THERE were an estimated two thousand professional footballers in Britain and just as many who could be called semiprofessionals. Soccer was shedding its skin. Decades earlier it had been a pastime confined to England's public schools, reserved for the scions of the upper middle class. It was played for fun and nothing more. But for a few years the prospect of easy and lucrative earnings had been luring boys from less affluent classes to the sport.

One way or another, the 1914–15 championship would be played. Everton would eventually win it. Of course, the championship was different from those that had come before; its aim had been to boost the country's morale, to take people's minds off the war and the war dead. That reasoning was questionable: news from the front came all the same and left little room for optimism. Indeed, soldiers were writing to their families, expressing disappointment with risking their lives in the trenches while their peers were playing soccer. And getting paid for it.

True, the Football Battalion met with some success, but ultimately the numbers wouldn't prove significant. During halftime at championship games, an official would position himself in the center of the field and invite fans to come down from the bleachers and affix their signatures to the enlistment sheet. It wasn't such a hot idea. The overwhelming majority was so skeptical that they asked King George V, the first sovereign to show an interest in soccer, to withdraw his patronage of the FA Cup. He didn't.

THE SCENE WAS later reconstructed in several short films about the first Christmas of the Great War. Morning, December 25. Out of the fog-shrouded German trench came a soldier. He raised his hands high in the air. Fear was written on his face: he knew he was an all-too-easy target for enemy snipers. The British kept their telescopes trained on him. They couldn't believe their eyes. Everyone was on alert—one nod and it was over for the soldier. "Stand down! He's unarmed." Those words saved the brave soldier's life. The Germans were given clearance: ten, a hundred, a thousand, came out of the trenches with their hands up. The British did likewise, first cautiously and then with confidence. Fear gave way to smiles. Hands were shaken. No-man's-land looked like a market square. Forgive me for asking, but if we're Saxons and you're Anglo-Saxons, why on earth are we shooting at each other?

It began with Christmas greetings, then gifts were exchanged. Gifts? Yes, those too. But it was not your average exchange of gifts; they made do with what they had. Among other things the Germans brought a keg of beer. The British returned the favor with Christmas pudding. Out came cigars and cigarettes—everyone at the front smoked to mitigate the unbearable smell of rotting corpses—and liquor and tins of meat and jam. One of the most coveted trophies was the uniform, or pieces of the uniform, belonging to an enemy soldier (if calling each other enemies made sense at that point). Captain Bruce Bairnsfather, who would go on to become one of Britain's most highly regarded cartoonists after the war, recalled spotting "a German officer, some sort of lieutenant

I should think, and being a bit of a collector, I intimated to him that I had taken a fancy to some of his buttons. We both then said things to each other which neither understood, and agreed to do a swap. I brought out my wire clippers and, with a few deft snips, removed a couple of his buttons and put them in my pocket. I then gave him two of mine in exchange." From small gestures like these, peace spread like wildfire. In every trench, soldiers talked, fraternized. A former barber offered his services to anyone in need of a quick cut. Friends or enemies, it made no difference.

"Any of you lot have a football?"

We don't know, and never will know, how the idea came about. But clearly that flurry of pats on the back and casual gift giving led someone to think of football, of *Fußball*, that marvelous game that had conquered the hearts of young people on both sides of the Channel.

A MATCH WAS played, maybe more than one. We must rely on the accounts of those who were there. Like Bertie Felstead, a Londoner, born in 1894. By his own admission, Felstead was no great shakes at soccer, but on that December 25, 1914, he didn't hesitate to accept an invitation to a pickup match. He often spoke about it after the war was over, over the many years he had left to live. He died in 2001, at the venerable age of 106, and a biographical profile of him appeared in the *News of the World Football Annual*, a kind of almanac of overseas soccer. That's not bad for someone who, apart from that Christmas, never played a match in his life. Even a

German club, MSV Duisburg, celebrated him on its website: "Instead of shooting, he celebrated and played. As long as soccer and people like Bertie exist, there will always be hope for humanity."

Felstead wasn't the only one who attested to the story of that match or others played that day. Mention of soccer being played appears in the testimony of Ernest "Ernie" Williams, who recounted taking part in a match in the middle of no-man's-land; it's hard to say whether it was the same match as Felstead's. Germany's Felstead was Johannes Niemann, a lieutenant in the 133rd Royal Saxon Regiment. In the diary Niemann kept during the war, he offers other details about that December 25. Because he wrote it down, one is inclined to believe him.

The one thing we know for sure is the date: Friday, December 25, 1914, Christmas Day. The details may be fuzzy, but on that day something important happened. Matches, or something like them, were played in a fifty-kilometer radius around Ypres. The ball started rolling after gifts were exchanged and soldiers were buried. Ceremonies had been planned on both sides, but the scale of the carnage meant soldiers resorted to digging mass graves and honoring the dead with one large funeral. The chaplains paid homage to the fallen in both languages. All that was left of those poor young men were military badges and wallets that would be jealously guarded until they could be handed over to their families. Where possible, there was musical accompaniment: Scottish bagpipes, German harmonicas.

But it isn't easy, as I've said, to reconstruct what transpired next, which is to say when they began playing. Let's try to establish a few things we do know. The match that Bertie Felstead and Johannes Niemann recounted was between, on one side, a group of English Lancashire Fusiliers with the support of some Welsh Fusiliers and Scottish Seaforth Highlanders, and, on the other, members of the German 133rd Royal Saxon Regiment. Apparently, a year earlier, some of the Germans had played in a tournament in Scotland, where they triumphed over Celtic, the champions. That previous encounter set the stage for what you might call a rematch.

The British supplied the ball, there were no refs, nor were there goals. Berets and helmets served as goalposts. The perimeter of the playing field was set by the soldiers watching the match. Accounts vary as to how long they played. As Felstead has it, "After about thirty minutes a vociferous major appeared, yelling, 'You came out to fight the Huns, not to make friends with them!'" But according to others, the game did not end until after an hour, signaled by an ominous cannon shot.

Half an hour, an hour: Does it matter? Far more suggestive was a detail found in several accounts of the time: whenever a player wound up on the ground, his opponents would be the first to help him to his feet, which was hardly an easy task given that their boots were caked with mud and their coats soaked by the rain. It was a powerful lesson in fair play. In his memoir, Johannes Niemann wrote, "The frozen ground made even the simplest play hard. The ball would go flying off and chasing after it was an ordeal. Yet everyone there, players and spectators, was filled with a peaceful sense of comradeship in the name of the sport."

Okay, but who won? *The New York Times* was the first to report the outcome, on January 1, citing an officer from a no less vaguely identified British regiment: the Germans won, though they didn't give the score. Lieutenant Niemann is more specific: 3–2 for the Saxon infantry. The same score appears in the diary of the Lancashire Fusiliers, with a footnote: the winning goal should have been overturned; someone was offside. When it comes to English and German soccer showdowns, nothing ever goes smoothly. Decades later it was Geoff Hurst's ghost goal at the 1966 World Cup final, and in 2010 it was Frank Lampard's unseen strike in South Africa.

Questions remain, one in particular: Can we be sure this is what really happened, that this and other games were in fact played? What if, on the contrary, it had all been imagined by young men who were losing their minds after seeing their comrades die? If they were still among us, Felstead and Niemann would probably not take kindly to such impertinent questions. Nor would Private Ernest Williams of the Cheshire Regiment, a veteran of that December 25 who told his story to the BBC in 1983, twenty days before he died: "[The ball] appeared from somewhere and I didn't know where . . . One fellow went in goal and then it was just a general kickabout. I should think there would be at least a couple of hundred taking part . . . I had a go at it—I was pretty good then, at nineteen."

We believe you, Ernest. Same as we believe Bertie Felstead and Johannes Niemann. Or at least we like to imagine how a single ball managed to grant them a moment's peace amid unrelenting tragedy.

"ON THE MORNING of December 26," wrote Michael Jürgs in *The Small Peace in the Great War*, "soldiers on either side seemed to be under the influence of a drug administered to them over the previous two days. A cocktail of music, soccer, prayers, quarrels. They wouldn't hear of picking up their weapons and starting to shoot again. The officers responded by threatening to shoot their own men if they didn't obey orders." That's the picture that comes into focus after Christmas soccer in no-man's-land.

To make matters worse, there was the post-match weather: temperatures rose, it began to rain again. The trenches gradually filled with water. There was the problem of mud, which in some cases reached as high as five feet. Then someone had an idea: accept that the war is starting again but pick up your rifle and fire—just above the height of any man. Aim a few feet above the enemy's head. A second lieutenant in the German army would later call it "a collective attempt to pull the stars down from the sky." It also served to slow down at least some of the carnage.

In January 1915 came the first military tribunals charging the men with cowardice in the face of the enemy. Many of the trials would never take place because the accused had died. The war would last another four years and eventually result in more than ten million deaths. Much of this was to the satisfaction of an Austrian corporal who, witnessing the Christmas truce, had admonished his fellow soldiers in the 16th Bavarian Reserve Infantry Regiment. According to him, "German and British soldiers shaking hands and singing Christmas carols ought to be strictly censured."

That corporal's name was Adolf Hitler.

CHAPTER 2

THE WHITE HORSE THAT SAVED WEMBLEY:
THE ENGLISH CUP AND EUROPE BETWEEN THE WARS

MATCH
Bolton Wanderers vs. West Ham United

FINAL SCORE
2–0

WHEN
April 28, 1923

WHERE
Wembley Stadium, London

EVERYONE WHO LOVES soccer owes a debt to Charles William Alcock, or so I think. Without him, the history of this beautiful sport would not have been the same. Or maybe—Who can say?—there'd be no history to speak of.

He was a nineteenth-century man, Alcock. Born in 1842 in Sunderland, he moved as a boy to southern England and attended Harrow School. This second detail proves important because Harrow School was one of the institutions that served as a laboratory for soccer as we know it. Before Alcock went to Harrow, people played the sport as they saw fit, more or less. From the number of players to physical contact—allowed if not encouraged—to the legal use of hands, the size of the pitch, and the rules of offsides, a fair amount of confusion reigned. Until, that is, Harrow School established what would become, with subsequent fine tuning, the ground rules of the game as we know them. Although progress *had* been made elsewhere, *vide* Cambridge.

Alcock was an excellent player. From 1870 to 1872, he represented England in five matches against Scotland, the first ever had FIFA (Fédération Internationale de Football Association) not discounted them—on the grounds that many of the Scots lived in and around London already. Therefore, Alcock's one recorded appearance on the national team goes back to another England–Scotland match, in 1875, which ended in a 2–2 tie. Though he didn't have a distinguished career, the young man had plenty of other things on his mind. In his early twenties, he contributed to the birth of the Football Association, the world's first soccer federation, which signed a charter on October 28, 1863, at London's mythic Freemasons' Tavern on Great Queen Street. While playing, he was studying ways to make a sport, still reliant on the whims of individual players, both comprehensible and enjoyable. Back then soccer was primarily—if not exclusively—a dribbling game, where anyone could plunge ahead and carry the ball upfield. Alcock helped turn it into a combination game, a team sport as we understand it today.

Newspapers of the time claimed he was the first footballer to have an offside whistle called, on March 31, 1866, in a match between the Wanderers, the team he played for, and the Sheffield Football Club. Whether or not the anecdote is true, he remains a crucial figure. He was also an umpire, cricketer, journalist, publisher, and, most importantly, served for twenty-five years as secretary of the Football Association, from 1870 to 1895. It was in this capacity that he came up with an idea that would take soccer one step further.

SOCCER WAS STILL in an embryonic stage, sustained exclusively by friendly matches. People played with no other objective than to kick the ball around a few times, knowing they'd play again another day. When and where was all that needed to be determined.

To keep the passion alive, something more was needed. Why not set up an official tournament? Why not put up a prize worth competing for? Alcock was reminded of his Harrow days. The school had four houses, each occupied by a certain number of students. Four houses, four teams. Each year there was a tournament to determine which house was the best, with two semifinals and a final match known in schoolyards of the day as the Cock House competition.

That was the idea that the Football Association would adopt in 1871. In that year, there were about fifty clubs affiliated with the federation. Many folded at the outset, others joined over time, and still others backed out in the thick of things, often because they were scared off by the costs of traveling for matches. The undertaking bordered on the impossible, but Coach Alcock would stop at nothing. In the end, fifteen teams would take the field. An odd number meant that one team would get a bye each round because, just as at Harrow School, the winning team would advance, and the losing team would be out of the competition. This model served as the blueprint for the English league's FA Cup.

THE BIG DAY was March 16, 1872. The first final was played at London's Kennington Oval, a facility that usually hosted Surrey County Cricket Club matches, a club where Charles Alcock himself presided as secretary. Or rather, secretary and player. This suggests that it must not have been that difficult to prepare the grounds for a sport other than cricket. Playing for the trophy in front of two thousand spectators were the Wanderers and the Royal Engineers. The Engineers won with a goal by Morton Betts, who for some reason played under the pseudonym "AH Chequer." On the field, among the winners, was the multifaceted Charles Alcock. Essentially, he wound up hoisting in the air the trophy that he himself had conceived.

During those years, soccer was growing at a steady clip, and the cup established by Alcock was continually evolving. The year 1882 marked the last victory of an amateur squad, the Old Etonians, made up of former students from prestigious Eton College. That was no small turning point, since soccer in England—the only country in the world where the game had a semblance of order—was about to become professionalized. That changed, if not everything, many things. The Football League was created, interest spiked, and money circulated. Now that there was the prospect of making money, boys from less affluent households began to play as well. The 1889 final between Preston North End and Wolverhampton drew 22,000 spectators to Kennington Oval. Sizeable, but nothing compared to the 110,000 in 1901 who came out to see Tottenham and Sheffield United play for the trophy at another stadium, Crystal Palace.

Charles Alcock wouldn't be around much longer to admire the growth of his tournament. He died in 1907, a few weeks after celebrating his sixty-fourth birthday. The mark he left behind is profound. By then soccer had taken root all over England, with every self-respecting town possessing at least two things: a church and a rectangular pitch where you could kick the ball around.

THIS GROWTH DID not come to a halt—Could it have been otherwise?—until the First World War; the very first year of conflict spelled the end of championships and sporting events. Having laid down its arms, the British Empire aimed to reassert itself as the global superpower. To re-establish ties with its far-flung overseas possessions and create jobs for veterans struggling to reintegrate into civilian life, a plan was hatched to stage the British Empire Exhibition, a global event whose stated aim was "to stimulate trade, strengthen bonds that bind mother Country to her Sister States and Daughters, to bring into closer contact the one with each other, to enable all who owe allegiance to the British flag to meet on common ground and learn to know each other."

They needed only to decide where to play the exhibition match. And they chose Wembley Park, an area northwest of London, in Middlesex. There was no shortage of land there. So much land, in fact, that the organizers hit upon an idea: in addition to the pavilions, why not build a soccer stadium? They'd call it Empire Stadium, and with 126,000 seats, it would become the centerpiece of the British Empire Exhibition. Once the match was over, the stadium would be dismantled. Or so residents thought. But history, as we shall see, had other plans.

The opening was scheduled for April 23, 1924. Work began two years earlier and proceeded so fast that, inside of twelve months, a year ahead of schedule, it was completed. That was when the Football Association came up with the idea of hosting the cup final at Wembley Stadium. They were just in time for the April 28, 1923, match between the Bolton Wanderers and West Ham United. Just three days to go, but it was worth a shot.

Choosing Wembley had its pros and cons. The three most recent finals had been played at Stamford Bridge, the home of Chelsea, and none had drawn a crowd. In 1922, spectators numbered just over fifty thousand, an alarming step backward from prewar attendance. Hence the troubling prospect of an Empire Stadium with many empty seats, a terrible sign for an exhibition scheduled to take place the following year. Despite these concerns, the venue didn't change. To avoid a public debacle, a decision was made to invest in a sweeping advertising campaign to lure fans to the stadium. The city was plastered with posters, and newspapers did their part, too. "Plenty of seats! Excellent views! Don't miss your chance!" was the pitch.

But that was the organizers' first mistake. They underestimated the scale of the event. There was no need to advertise the match as much as they did. It was, after all, a cup final, and it was being played in a brand-new stadium—the largest in the world. Moreover, April 28 turned out to be a decidedly un-London-like day with summery weather, and people were eager to spend it outdoors. On top of that, taking the field was West Ham, a team from the capital with an enormous fan base. Given the tight schedule and the impossibility of selling seats in advance, the ticket offices even remained open on match day. The London Underground would later say that it issued 241,000 tickets to Wembley on the day of the final. And that's not counting fans who traveled there without a ticket, or those who chose to go by bus or private car or even on foot. Nor were the premises equipped to maintain public order.

AT 11:30 A.M., three and a half hours before the first whistle, the gates swung open. Things began to escalate around 1:00 p.m. as more and more fans elbowed their way to seats in the stands. One victim of overcrowding was the coach carrying the Bolton players, which was forced to stop a mile from the stadium, unable to get any closer. The players hopped off and went the rest of the way on foot. It soon became obvious just how unprepared the stadium ushers and police forces were. At 1:45 p.m., a decision was made to close the gates, but it was like trying to hold back the tide. People did as they pleased, scaling the gate or making a beeline for the stands, even though the stadium was already filled beyond capacity. Among the first to realize conditions were degenerating were the journalists, who arrived at their seats to discover they were occupied by spectators who'd never written a snippet of news.

The remaining multitudes had no choice but to head over to the playing field and watch the game from there. The numbers are still shocking. Police reports say there were 300,000 people; other sources say 250,000—either way, double the stadium's capacity. It puts one in mind of a huge impending tragedy.

The account of one spectator, George Kerr, is worth pulling from the archives: "When I arrived at the stadium, I saw the turnstiles had been built into wooden structures that were about eight feet high, the turnstiles themselves were locked and deserted but bodies were climbing over them like monkeys and I quickly followed suit . . . I got behind the crowd and soon was being pushed forward by others who got behind me. I was literally pushed into the ground."

Postpone the match? It was a possibility. But how would the three hundred thousand people crowding the stadium react? Better go ahead and play. West Ham proposed making the final a friendly and awarding the cup another time. But that wouldn't solve the problem. The risk of visitors being trampled was too high. We're talking tens of thousands of people—on the sidelines!

At 2:45 p.m., King George V turned up at the stadium. Assuming the match would be played, he would be the one to bestow the cup on the winners. The King was told to return to Buckingham Palace. For safety concerns, obviously. But staunch soccer fan that he was, King George decided to remain, safety be damned. His appearance on the royal stage tempered the mood for a few minutes. The fans chanted, "God save the King." It would have been a moving moment had it solved the problem at hand. The players didn't take the field until 3:10 p.m., after the scheduled start time. They tried to persuade the crowd to back up, but to no avail, not least because the fans were stunned to be standing so close to their idols. According to one bizarre anecdote, Bolton's center forward, David Jack, felt a tap on his shoulder. It was his brother, whom he hadn't seen in six years.

GEORGE SCOREY WAS a mounted policeman. He was forty years old and had lived many lives. At the start of the new century, he had been a trumpeter with the English troops in the Second Anglo-Boer War, and he had once escorted the Russian royal family on their visit to Britain. At the outbreak of the First World War, he was sent to the Western Front and fought in the first two battles of Ypres. Back home, he was assigned to the mounted branch of London's Metropolitan Police, which would enable him to pursue his passion for playing the trumpet.

On that day, April 28, Scorey was not on duty. Or at least not at the stadium. But he responded to the emergency call as the situation deteriorated. With his horse Billy, his trusted companion, he posted outside the stadium before being redirected to the pitch. About ten horses were engaged, all black except for Billy, who had a gray coat, though in photos of the time he appears snow-white.

That "white horse" would become the emblem of the 1923 FA Cup final. Scorey would tell the story a thousand times:

> As Billy picked his way onto the field, all I could see was a sea of heads. It looked an impossible task but . . . I knew the game had to go ahead somehow. My horse was wonderful, gently easing folk back with his nose and tail until we had pushed the crowd over one of the goal lines. We continued

> up the touchlines until a small number of people became a bit stubborn. "Don't you want to see the game?" I shouted above the noise. "Yes," they replied. "Well, so do I. Now those of you in front join hands." Then I gave the order to heave! And they went back, inch by inch, until the touchline was cleared. Then I told them to sit down, and with the help of my colleagues, the pitch itself was gradually cleared. I'm positive that any credit I received was due to Billy. Perhaps because he was white, Billy commanded more attention, but, more than that, he seemed to understand exactly what was wanted of him.

It may seem unlikely that a horse and rider could single-handedly avert a colossal tragedy. But photos from that day appear to prove just that. We ought to bear in mind that the other quadrupeds helped out, too, even if they had the misfortune of being less striking in the black-and-white photos of the time—and to the collective imagination. They weren't the stars of that unprecedented show but walk-on parts.

Once order had been restored, the match could finally get underway. It was 3:45 p.m., forty-five minutes past the original start time, but that was the least of their problems. Referee David Asson convened captains Joe Smith and George

Key and must have said something like, "Look, it's just me and two of my linesmen here versus two hundred thousand people, maybe more. If you guys don't lend us a hand, I don't know how we're getting out of this." Bolton immediately took the lead on a throw-in by West Ham defender Jack Tresadern, who got trapped in the crowd and couldn't get back to the pitch, leaving his teammates outnumbered. Bolton regained control of the ball, and David Jack—the player who had just been reunited with his brother—scored. Jack's ball hit a spectator posted behind the goal. The poor fan was unconscious on the ground.

1–0 at the half. In a normal match, the two teams would return to the locker room for an afternoon cup of tea. But this was no normal match. The players found themselves facing a human wall and could do nothing but stand. That explains why halftime lasted just five minutes. Once play resumed it took Bolton another eight minutes to pull ahead 2–0. The goal, scored by Jack Smith, was contested. West Ham claimed the ball hit the goalpost and bounced back into play. "I'll allow it," replied the referee, who believed a spectator kicked the ball back only after it had crossed the goal line. West Ham insisted that one of the spectators passed the ball to Ted Vizard, who made the assist to Smith. Asson wouldn't listen and told everyone to resume play.

It was two goals too many for West Ham to mount a comeback. After all, they were a second division team, albeit one on the brink of their first historic promotion to the top tier. Bolton, which had played two cup finals and lost both, was the more seasoned team. It handled the situation and took few if any risks until the final whistle. The rest of the match was dominated by protests from the losing side. The one who really lost his cool was the assistant coach, Charlie Paynter: "It was that white horse thumping its big feet into the pitch that made it hopeless. Our wingers were tumbling all over the place, tripping up in great ruts and holes."

Poor Billy—rather than thanked for his service he was blamed for West Ham's defeat . . .

David Jack, the player who scored the first goal, would be the MVP of that final. Three years later, in exchange for £10,890, he'd leave Bolton to join Arsenal, then coached by Herbert Chapman, the mastermind behind the so-called system. It was the costliest transfer in the early history of English soccer. According to reports, Bolton asked for an even larger payout, but Chapman convinced the other side to lower its offer by plying them with gin and tonics.

The final was in the books, but the toll had yet to be calculated. How many people were injured? Just shy of a thousand spectators sought medical attention, the vast majority reporting only minor injuries. It was a miracle, or maybe the masterwork of that white horse, which deserved all the praise the papers heaped on it.

News of the World dubbed Scorey the "Wellington of Wembley." And the party dragged through the mud was the Football Association, which eventually decided to allocate 10 percent of the proceeds to all those ticketed fans who failed to make it to their assigned seats. The London authorities set up a commission of inquiry to shed light on what went wrong. Changes were eventually made: taller fences, more entrance gates, more clearly marked sections, and a moratorium against selling tickets on match day. George Scorey was awarded free admission to all future FA Cup finals, but he wouldn't be seen in the vicinity again. He never had cared much for soccer, and that nightmarish afternoon did absolutely nothing to excite his interest.

Plans to demolish Empire Stadium were scrapped and Wembley Stadium would go on to become one of the sport's most iconic arenas. The high point of its one-hundred-year history will forever remain England's victory at the 1966 World Cup final. Music buffs remember it as the stadium that hosted the European half of Live Aid, the legendary 1985 concert organized by Bob Geldof that saw Elton John, Freddie Mercury, Paul McCartney, U2, and other legends share the stage. It was demolished at the turn of the century, but only to make room for a new state-of-the-art stadium. Today, the 1923 structure has been replaced with an ultramodern facility. To reach it, spectators must cross a footbridge over the station tracks. The bridge did not have a name until 2005, when soccer fans were polled to choose an individual to name it after. In the running were Alf Ramsey, Bobby Charlton, and Geoff Hurst—the coach and two of the most charismatic players of England's 1966

World Cup champions. The honor could have gone to any one of them. Instead, a plurality of fans—34 percent—voted to pay tribute to Billy and, by extension, to the man who rode him on April 28, 1923. Were it not for those two, that day would most likely be remembered as one of the darkest in soccer history.

CHAPTER 3

THE GREAT REFUSAL:
SINDELAR, ANSCHLUSS, AND THE NAZIS

MATCH
Austria vs. Germany

FINAL SCORE
2–0

WHEN
April 3, 1938

WHERE
Prater Stadium, Vienna

My father always told me, "You're the best of your generation. But remember: a long time ago there was a player who was better than you—Matthias Sindelar. He was the greatest of all." And I believe him, because my father understood soccer.
—Herbert Prohaska, June 2008, RAI Sport

MATTHIAS SINDELAR WAS born in 1903. Austria was still an empire, albeit an unstable one, and his family lived in Iglau (today Jihlava), a small town in Moravia 125 miles outside the capital. The prospects for achieving financial stability weren't great, so the Sindelars moved to sprawling Vienna when Matthias was not yet three years old. They went to live in Favoriten, a neighborhood far from the luxurious city center, where the tenements were affordable, living conditions were modest, and the overriding ambition was to put food on the table. There was little in the way of entertainment, at least for adults. The youth, on the other hand, knew how to have fun: all you needed was to tie a couple of rags together hard enough and you got yourself a homemade soccer ball. There they played morning to night, wherever they could—even in the streets, down which the first cars had yet to hazard—and became the bane of every mother's existence.

Matthias could handle that rough-and-ready ball; indeed, he was the best at it. Every night he came home to 101 Quellenstrasse dead tired but alive and well. Ordinary as it seems, the street is significant in the history of soccer, Austrian and otherwise. Around the same time, the Bican family settled at number 87. Their second son, Josef, was born when Matthias was ten years old. Given their age difference, Josef and Matthias wouldn't play together in the neighborhood, but later, at the 1934 World Cup, both men would don the Austrian jersey and make up for lost time. Yes, the boy from 87 Quellenstrasse would grow up to become a professional soccer player. And what a player he was! In his long career, Josef Bican would score 805 goals in official matches, a record he'd hold for almost eighty years, until Cristiano Ronaldo came along.

IN ADULTHOOD, BICAN would prove to be a peculiar figure, famous for his eccentricities. According to some sources, whenever he traveled for reasons other than a match or practice, he would book two taxis: the first to ride in himself, dressed as if for a wedding, and the second for his cane and hat.

Although teeming with stories of questionable reliability—as we shall soon see— Matthias Sindelar's biography contains none of the dandyish behavior of a Bican. Quite the opposite. He was orphaned in the middle of the First World War, after his father died in Italy during one of the battles of the Isonzo in 1917. Putting food on the table required rolling up your sleeves, so at just fourteen years old the boy had to hurry up and learn the basics of the coachbuilding trade. He went to work, but he never gave up his great passion. He joined the youth league of Hertha Vienna, one of the many teams in the capital. Watching him converse with the ball was thrilling; he seemed to be playing a different game than the other twenty-one boys on the field, teammates and opponents. From Hertha he graduated to Wiener Amateur, a club that would shortly thereafter become Vienna. It was, along with Rapid and Admira, among the best of the best.

In the 1920s and 1930s, there was one thing that set Vienna apart from other countries: soccer was a social phenomenon that transcended the sport itself. Not only did it draw tens of thousands of people to stadiums, but, more importantly, it got people talking about it long after the ninety minutes of play. Those attending matches talked soccer and so did those milling about public squares, where rudimentary loudspeakers were set up to broadcast news on the radio. Soccer was even talked about in drawing rooms, where the bourgeoisie and aristocracy nibbled on pastries and sipped tea. It became a topic of conversation on par with the latest play or movie or book. It was thanks at least in part to the exploits of Matthias Sindelar and his style of play, which elevated soccer to an art form. Today, we would label *Das Kind aus Favoriten* ("the boy from Favoriten") a "false nine"—a central striker in name only. He liked to switch things up, to paint with the ball. Indeed, some people compared him to a painter, others to Mozart or a chess player who can see three or four moves ahead. Those paying close attention from the stands could be forgiven for thinking he was less intent on scoring than on creating paths to score.

And to think that at age twenty he had already hit a critical snag in his career. A fall was to blame. In a bathtub, according to some. According to others, in an empty pool. Whatever the truth, he injured his meniscus, which for a soccer player a hundred years ago was a career killer. But then Sindelar met a surgeon, Dr. Hans Spitzy, who decided to operate. No athlete had ever had the surgery. In a sense, Sindelar was a guinea pig. But what choice did he have? He wanted to keep playing no matter what. The surgery was successful, and from then on, whenever he took the field, he would wear a knee guard to protect his right leg. Teammates, opponents, and spectators would never lay eyes on Dr. Spitzy's reconstructed knee. What they would see were the marvels of the boy from Moravia. It is at this point that he became "der Papierene," the Paper Man: delicate but extraordinarily beautiful to watch.

THE 1920S WERE not an age of intercontinental and world tournaments. But national teams from Central Europe had been competing since 1927 in what is called, in the holy annals of soccer, the International Cup. Italy, Austria, Czechoslovakia, Hungary, and Switzerland took part. It was a good group of teams, if small, since the British representatives, with a healthy dose of arrogance, opted out of official play and only competed in a handful of friendly matches. Eventually, the International Cup became the closest thing to a European championship tournament.

Austria's manager was Hugo Meisl. Meisl was an authority in the world of soccer: before coaching the national team he was a referee and journalist, and later became General Secretary of the Football Federation. He spoke many languages, crisscrossed Europe to keep up to speed with the latest developments in the game, and befriended his Italian counterpart Vittorio Pozzo. Elegance was Meisl's defining feature. Depending on the season, he always marched on to the field in a jacket and tie or a hat and overcoat.

Digging through the archives I came across an interview in which Meisl describes Austrian soccer as "characterized by an openness to different styles. We closely follow how other countries play the game, take the best from each, and dispense with the worst. What is left we combine with the elegance and lightness of those born and raised in Vienna." His statement may sound neutral, but Herr Meisl is actually taking a swipe at Britain's embrace of a physical game, a style of play that doesn't care for refined footballers who avoid physical contact. Which is to say Matthias Sindelar's style of play. Der Papierene made his national debut at the age of twenty-three. He played four games and scored as many goals, just to demonstrate his talent, and then mysteriously fell through the cracks. Over the next four years he would take the field a mere three times—three out of a total of twenty-eight games that Austria played.

The history of soccer is full of that kind of thing, where players who deserve to be on their national teams are for one reason or another spurned by coaches. But Sindelar was a special case: the boy from the streets of Favoriten was Austria's strongest player, no ifs, ands, or buts about it. In his mid-twenties he had already won a championship and two national cups with Austria Vienna. That's a major accomplishment, especially if you consider the stiff competition from Rapid and Admira. The press—sports journals and otherwise—sung his praises, but Hugo Meisl continued to ignore them.

Then came May 1931. Vienna was awaiting Scotland, a national team that had gone undefeated outside of Britain. The match was all anyone could talk about, in the streets and in the cafés. Meisl was a habitue of one such place: the Ringcafé. Journalists knew it and often sought him out there to talk soccer. Or rather, more than talk, to lock horns. Even then the coach wouldn't back down. But days out from the Scotland match the situation was in danger of deteriorating. The team was in crisis mode, and the journalists cornered him and demanded he put Sindelar on the field. Meisl finally gave in. He took out a pen and paper and set down his lineup. One by one he listed the names of the eleven players, the last being that of Austria Vienna's golden boy. "There, now you have your *Schmieranski*-team," he blurted to the press. *Schmieranski* comes from the word *Schmierer*, meaning "hack" or "scribbler." Here's your team, you pen pushers. Despite his choice of words, Meisl had surrendered.

AUSTRIA VS. SCOTLAND began at 5:45 p.m. on May 16, at Vienna's Hohe Warte Stadium. Forty thousand people were in attendance. It wasn't a match; it was a blowout. Hugo Meisl's boys won 5–0, with virtually no resistance. A distracted observer could have been forgiven for thinking the teams were from different divisions, the match a preseason friendly. By far the best player on the field was Matthias Sindelar. He scored the fifth goal and delighted fans with plays that boggled the mind.

Eight days later came another friendly, this time against Germany. Austria was playing away, in Berlin, but that matters little. In fact, Sindelar and his teammates scored one more goal than they did against Scotland, and once again they conceded none. That was when the Viennese newspapers dubbed them the Wunderteam, the team of miracles, a label that didn't sit well with Meisl. At the mere mention of Wunderteam, the coach would lambast the press: "The idiots who came up with that name should be hanged. It's a word that haunts me. What Wunderteam? What miracle? There are no miracles, especially not in soccer. To hell with whoever came up with that stupid name!"

But Meisl would have to live with it. His team was synonymous with Wunderteam and would remain so. To find a defeat you'd have to jump ahead to December 7, 1932, and it is an outlier. Austria traveled to London to face off against England. The anticipation was such that Vienna's parliament interrupted its proceedings to allow members to listen to the match on the radio. Before kickoff, the Duke of Kent greeted both teams but was most intrigued by the visitors. When he got to the defender Karl Sesta, he said something to the effect of "playing soccer sure is a nice job." Sesta listened to the interpreter and replied, "Maybe, Duke, but your job isn't so bad either." Which is to say, "If you think we have it easy, take a look at your job!" Then the match was on, and it was pure spectacle. The English ran away with it; the Austrians tried to catch up. The final score was 4–3 in the home team's favor, but the losers received most of the cheers. (It was like England vs. Italy, 1934, when Rome's world champions, with ten men on the field, came back from 3–0 down to finish 3–2, earning them the nickname the Lions of Highbury.) Sindelar scored the second Austrian goal, starting from midfield and cutting a swath through half of England. Referee John Langenus, who also presided over the 1930 World Cup final between Uruguay and Argentina, remarked, "Sindelar's goal was a masterpiece, which no one else—no one before him and no one after him—could possibly have scored against opponents as good as the English."

Sindelar was inundated with contract proposals from half the First Division, England's top league. The most attractive came from Herbert Chapman, the manager rewriting soccer history on the Arsenal bench. He supposedly offered the Austrian up to £40,000, an enormous amount at the time. "Nein danke," said Sindelar—to Chapman and everyone else. He was happy in Vienna. And besides, there was the issue of his meniscus, which he could tear at any moment in a league as physical as the one across the Channel. Not to mention the language obstacle. The future had looked kindly on his decisions, at least where sports were concerned: with Vienna he would twice win the Central European Cup, a progenitor of the Champions League. In Austria's capital, Sindelar was a living legend, earning a comfortable living and already contemplating his next move. He wanted to open one of those cafés where people linger late into the night and talk soccer. It was an idea to keep in his back pocket—a dream in a drawer, as we say in Italian.

1934 WAS THE year of the Italian World Cup. Austria arrived the favorite, or at least among the favorites. It eliminated France and Hungary, and in the semifinals in Milan squared off against Vittorio Pozzo's Azzurri in a match that felt like a premature final. It wasn't much of a show. More grappling than soccer, so to speak. And Sindelar endured the brunt of it, being manhandled by Azzurri midfielder Luis Monti. The Wunderteam was too technical to withstand the physicality of their opponents, and, in the end, Italy stole the match out from under them. Enrique Guaita's decisive goal raised eyebrows; Giuseppe Meazza may very well have pushed goalkeeper Peter Platzer.

That was the end of Sindelar's World Cup. Instead of playing in the final for third place against Germany, the Paper Man wound up in the hospital. And this is when the pivotal figure in the later years of Sindelar's life appeared on the scene: Camilla Castagnola, who, depending on the version of the story, was either a nurse or a teacher, an Italian or an Austrian of Italian descent, a lover or just a friend. But most importantly she was Jewish, a detail that will take on great significance. Nello Governato discusses this at length in *La partita dell'addio* (The Goodbye Match), a fictionalized biography that, despite its excellent reconstruction of historical events, isn't bound by the goalposts of reality.

When did Matthias and Camilla meet? Governato places their meeting in the weeks after the World Cup, when Sindelar was still in Italy recovering. They met under the lights of a hospital ward (an enticing thought, but bear in mind it belongs to a novel). Another version of the story, corroborated by Austrian sources, has the pair meeting much later, in the last months or even final weeks of Sindelar's life. It's no use trying to get the dates straight, not least because records are few, fragmentary, and often contradictory. What we know for sure is that, even after the Italian World Cup, Sindelar continued to delight the Viennese with his feats on the field. It's just too bad his body had sustained so many injuries and the effects of aging. The next World Cup was scheduled for 1938, when the Paper Man was thirty-seven. Old for soccer, perhaps prohibitively so. But it wasn't just that. Sindelar sensed that something was changing in Vienna. Nazi Germany had its eye on neighboring Austria. A word was hovering in the air, keeping people up at night: Anschluss.

Most startled was the city's large Jewish community. One member of that community was the president of Austria Vienna, Michael Schwarz, who was like a father to Sindelar, one of many around whom the Nazis would make scorched earth. The day came when Schwarz was forced out of his post and took refuge in Switzerland. Sindelar saluted him, saying, "Whenever I am lucky enough to see you again, Mr. President, I will always say good morning." The Anschluss was an objective that the Austrian-born Hitler had long had in his sights. He had tried to annex Austria before, in 1934, but the strong response from Western powers persuaded him to give it up. Four short years later, everything had changed. The Führer mobilized Austria's Nazis and forced Chancellor von Schuschnigg to resign. On March 11, 1938, the government, led by the Nazi Arthur Seyss-Inquart, officially called for the intervention of the German army "to save the country from chaos." In a matter of hours, the Reich army had entered Austrian territory and annexed it to Germany, a dress rehearsal for what would soon happen in other parts of Europe.

As a result, the nation of Austria ceased to exist and, along with it, the national soccer team. The Nazis wanted Austria, including Austrian sports, to be *judenfrei*, free of Jews. But first they had to stage, as propaganda had it, a "reconciliation match." It was the last match for Austria, though that was no longer its name; now it was known as Ostmark, or the eastern province, and it would face off against Altreich, or the old kingdom (Germany, of course). The match was to be played at Vienna's Prater Stadium on April 3, 1938, a week before the referendum that would sanction the Anschluss. From then on, it was as if there were two Matthias Sindelars, or at least two different accounts of him. The Paper Man is consistently on the field, alongside his great friend Karl Sesta. The one person missing is Hugo Meisl, who had died of a heart attack a few months earlier. According to some sources, Sindelar saw the match as a battle against Nazism. And the battle began with his uniform: he wore a red jersey and white shorts in honor of his nation and the national team that had just been erased from existence.

There was no camaraderie on the pitch. The Austrians humiliated their adversaries by literally hiding the ball or refusing to score when the most attractive opportunity presented itself, until, in the second half, they decided to get serious. Then came the goals: one by Sindelar inside the box, another by Sesta from midfield. The Germans were stone-faced, and under the grandstand, in front of party leaders, the Paper Man celebrated with an exuberance more South American than Austrian. At the end of the match, everyone gave the Nazi salute. Everyone, that is, but Sindelar and Sesta.

That's one version of events. According to another, they wore their usual jerseys and no one threw down the gauntlet. At the entrance, some players displayed a banner that read SPORTSMEN VOTE YES, a reference to the upcoming referendum. Was Sindelar among them? So it seems. And after the goal, no one mocked the Nazi hierarchy. A jubilant Sindelar simply turned to his friends in the stands. There is no point in trying to confirm either version: the newspapers of the time are unreliable, riddled with propaganda, and there are no surviving witnesses.

1938 WAS ALSO the year of the World Cup in France. Austria qualified by narrowly beating Latvia, but then what happened, happened. The national team was disbarred, and its best players sent to Germany to boost its roster. But not all of them went; Sindelar refused. Coach Sepp Herberger visited him at home but failed to change his mind. Many years later, Herberger recalled their meeting: "He told me about his knee and his wish to retire. He acted like the gracious man I knew him to be. I gathered that he had other reasons for not wanting to play, so I let the matter go." What other reasons did he have? Herberger never elaborated, but one can imagine Sindelar's displeasure at not being able to don the jersey of his national team. Or perhaps it was something deeper, like his aversion to a regime that had wiped Austria off the map. That's how Germany's *Sport Bild* sees it. Recently, the magazine suggested that Sindelar justified his refusal by saying, "I will never take the field for this entity that calls itself Germany and is gobbling up Europe." At the World Cup, "great" Germany—and a few reinforcements labeled Ostmark—didn't get far. The team was eliminated in the first round by Switzerland, coached by Karl Rappan, one of the fathers of *catenaccio*—a tactical system in soccer centered on defense—and an Austrian himself.

But there is one moment in Sindelar's brief life that helps shed light on his character, especially on his attitude toward the Nazis. In 1938, the Paper Man realized his dream of opening a café to ensure a secure future once he had hung up his cleats. This was at the height of "Aryanization," when Jews were being dispossessed of their property—property that wound up in Aryan hands. Having gotten his papers in order, Sindelar took over the Annahof café from Leopold Drill, a Jew who would later die in the Theresienstadt concentration camp. He purchased it for twenty thousand reichsmark, a steal if you consider that in 1937 alone, Drill had earned four times that amount.

Was he doing the famous champion a favor? In exchange for what? In 2013, the Vienna daily *Die Presse* wrote: "The National Socialist Party leadership carried out Sindelar's request, having found nothing objectionable about the party member's political views." A party member? Sindelar? That was odd because two weeks earlier, when asked if he belonged to the party, he'd said no. Could things have really changed in a few short days? Any suspicion that Sindelar was pro-Nazi has long been rejected by Norbert Lopper, the postwar secretary of Austria Vienna: "Sindelar knew the previous owner well. Clearly, he wanted to help him out, so he decided to take over the business lest it fall into the hands of outsiders."

Considering all this, the benefit of the doubt is warranted. The four historians who wrote *Ein Fussballverein aus Wien* (A Football Club from Vienna), a book about Austria Vienna under the Nazis, had this to say about the affair: "We cannot make a moral judgment about Sindelar's actions. Key information is missing, like whether the player actively participated in bargaining down the price. Nor is it known whether he was aware of the criminal methods used by the Nazis to pressure the owner. It is a matter of shedding light on the process of Aryanization, specifically on what role his having been a public figure may have played."

On the morning of January 23, 1939, gestapo agents and firefighters charged into the apartment at 3 Annagasse and found a man lying lifeless beside a woman in desperate condition. Shortly after came the shocking discovery that the dead man was Matthias Sindelar and the woman lying in bed, the owner of the apartment, was Camilla Castagnola. She too would die a few hours later, having never regained consciousness. According to the report, the cause was carbon monoxide poisoning from a faulty stove. Some speculate that it was a problem with the chimney, but that is unlikely, given the first to rule out that theory were the firefighters. The case file disappeared, the bodies were cremated, and it became impossible to learn the truth. Rumors abounded. It was an accident. No, suicide. Suicide? Please, it was the gestapo. They murdered him. According to the most disturbing theory, his refusal to play in the World Cup in France and his failure to give the Nazi salute after the match of April 3, 1938, had something to do with it.

Everyone feels entitled to their opinion. In 1999, the *Neue Kronen-Zeitung* dusted off an article by Robert Brum, a journalist and friend of Sindelar, written immediately after the tragedy and titled "She Handed Him the Hemlock." Brum claims that Sindelar stumbled into a fatal love affair that ended with his being poisoned. To support his argument, Brum claims there was a half-full bottle of cognac on the bedside table whose contents were never analyzed. There are also the verses of writer Friedrich Torberg, a great admirer of Sindelar:

> He knew little about life
> besides soccer. He lived,
> because he had to live,
> through soccer and for soccer . . .
> Until one day another opponent
> appeared in his way . . .
> He foresaw a gas leak
> would be his fate.

According to Torberg, Sindelar was a young man with limited prospects who decided to end it all because he believed he would lose Camilla, a Jew whose own fate was sealed. A theory that doesn't make sense if the two were just friends. In any case, the figure of Matthias Sindelar appears harder to pin down than previously thought, especially his attitude toward the Nazis. Most people still believe he opposed them, though their conviction has waned over the years. Questions remain, questions that can't be answered, like those posed by another of Austria's great soccer players, Herbert Prohaska. His words prove that the mystery surrounding Sindelar is destined to remain a mystery: "Who was Sindelar? A hero of the resistance, as so many intellectuals have hailed him, or a man who, like most people back then, adapted to circumstances? And even if he was, like so many others, looking out for his own interests, who are we, eighty years on, to judge him?"

CHAPTER 4

THE GOAL THAT COULD HAVE SAVED THEM:
"VELENO" LORENZI, POSTWAR ITALY, AND THE GRANDE TORINO TRAGEDY

MATCH
Inter vs. Torino

FINAL SCORE
0–0

WHEN
April 30, 1949

WHERE
San Siro Stadium, Milan

AT THE LAST moment it turns out Valentino Mazzola has come down with a severe fever after suffering from a sore throat. Torino's trainers decide he cannot take the field against Inter. He will most likely be replaced by the Hungarian Schubert or Bongiorni.

This news is buried on page 2 of the April 30, 1949, issue of *Corriere della Sera*. In a capsule. Torino's captain will miss the fifth to last league game scheduled for that same day, a heavy absence at this pivotal moment in the season. Torino's Granata has a four-point advantage over Inter Milan. A loss will, for all intents and purposes, put Italy's Serie A championship, the Scudetto, back in play. It is unheard of in postwar tournaments, which have all been dominated by Torino.

This is where the story of the greatest disaster to befall Italian soccer begins. It's a story of grief, yes, but also, as we shall see, one of regret for what could have been.

VALENTINO MAZZOLA, BORN and bred in the town of Cassano d'Adda, was enormously sorry to miss the showdown in Milan. San Siro was, after all, San Siro, possibly soon to be *his* stadium: there was more talk of trading Granata's No. 10 to Inter, the Nerazzurri. Inter also represented Mazzola's friend Benito Lorenzi. The two had met on the national team and despite different temperaments held each other in high regard. Valentino had been one of Italy's leaders whereas Lorenzi was a newcomer trying to make his name. Thus far he hadn't made much headway—just one appearance in a friendly against Spain. But Valentino stuck his neck out for his young colleague, whispering a few good words in the ear of Ferruccio Novo, the head honcho of the Technical Commission and coach of Italy's national team, the Azzurri. For the record, Novo was also the president of Torino. One assumes it didn't take much for Valentino Mazzola to be granted an audience.

Benito Lorenzi was known as "Veleno," or Poison, a nickname that speaks volumes. He earned it as a child in

Borgo a Buggiano, near Pistoia, where he'd gotten into trouble. And that didn't change in adulthood, despite his growth on the field. In 1947, after scoring two goals during his second appearance for Inter, he taunted his Juventus opponents so much that one of them, the world champion Pietro Rava, set out with the intention of punching him, but with feline grace Lorenzi dodged, and Rava wound up striking another Inter player, Bruno Quaresima, who just happened to be passing by. Quaresima was out cold.

Lorenzi was a loose cannon on the field, a boyish man off it. That April 30, 1949, Mazzola would have gladly shaken hands with his young colleague and perhaps used the opportunity to ask him about the mood at Inter. But nothing came of it.

There was another match scheduled for Torino. The team had to fly to Lisbon for a friendly with Benfica on Tuesday, May 3. It was to be the farewell match for the team captain, Francisco José Ferreira. The previous February in Genoa, he and Mazzola had spoken during another friendly between Italy and Portugal, which the Azzurri won 4–1. Ferreira was hoping to end his career playing Torino, one of the most admired teams in the world, and his wish was being granted. All the proceeds were to go to him, minus the travel expenses incurred by the club from Piedmont. President Novo set just one condition: his team could not lose to Inter Milan. The margin of advantage over the Nerazzurri could not be narrowed.

In other words, they needed to tie at San Siro or, better

still, win. Otherwise they'd be staying home. The battle for the *scudetto* took precedence, all well-wishes and apologies to captain Ferreira.

TO UNDERSTAND THE goings-on of football back then, some historical context is in order. It was 1949, four years after the war, which had left a landscape of death and destruction in its wake. Necessities were scarce. To travel from Rome to Naples by train took seven hours, from Rome to Milan over thirty. Some wounds did not heal easily, including those of a social nature; there were people who fought fascism and people who benefitted from fascism, and those groups found themselves sharing offices and classrooms.

Sports helped. Torino had become everyone's team, the symbol of a country desperate to get back on its feet and return to normalcy. But soccer wasn't the only sport. Italy was also basking in the glory of cyclists Fausto Coppi and Gino Bartali. Football and cycling—the two cornerstones of postwar European athletics. In 1948, Bartali took home the Tour de France just days after an assassination attempt on the leader of Italy's Communist Party, Palmiro Togliatti. The country had skidded to the brink of a civil war that some believed had been avoided in part because of Bartali's triumph. That may be overstating things, yet clearly the news from France must have helped divert people's attention from far more serious and dramatic matters at home.

At the time of the assassination attempt on Togliatti, and Bartali's Tour de France victory, Torino was in Brazil. They were scheduled to play friendlies against the Corinthians, Palmeiras, Portuguesa, and São Paulo. A bona fide world tour, an event that for the era felt out of the ordinary. But we can't measure it by today's metrics: in those years moving from one continent to another was a nearly impossible undertaking. Still, the Granatas enthusiastically accepted the invitation, for money, maybe, as well as the applause of those—many of Italian origin—who couldn't wait to see in person a team whose exploits were known as far away as South America.

For a team from Turin that had toured the length and breadth of Brazil, a trip to Portugal must have seemed like little more than a day out. But first they had to earn the trip to Lisbon. Ferruccio Novo had made himself clear.

Born in 1897, Novo became Torino's president in 1939. His family owned an industrial leather goods factory. Nothing on the scale of FIAT, let alone companies outside Turin, but enough to own a Serie A club. To devote himself full-time to soccer, Novo handed off management of the company to his brother Mario.

Juventus ruled the city at the time, having won five consecutive championships, but that didn't deter Novo. If he couldn't rival them financially, he'd compete with shrewd management. He surrounded himself with trusted collaborators with whom he planned every single move, starting with trading players.

Valentino Mazzola, for example, became a Granata in 1942. Until that time, he had played for Venice, a city he came to after being drafted into the navy. When he heard about the tryouts, he turned up at the pitch barefoot; apparently, he didn't have enough money for a pair of cleats. Nonetheless, officials in Venice only needed to see him kick the ball four times before signing him—and providing him with decent footwear. Alongside Mazzola was his devoted friend Ezio Loik. The year before, the pair had practically won the Italian Cup by themselves. Novo didn't think twice and secured them for the sum of 1,250,000 lire. Juventus also wanted to sign them, only its envoys stopped at nine hundred thousand, convinced it would be enough.

Torino was innovative on the field, too. It practiced the *sistema*, a formation that became popular in 1930s England, but that Italy had always struggled to adopt. Previously, Pozzo had won two World Cups using a tactic called the *metodo*, where two defenders would play behind three midfielders. In the *sistema*, however, a midfielder drops back to the line of wingbacks, who spread out to form a three-man defense. It was also called "WM," after the formation from top to bottom, attack to defense. But Torino won not because of the formation it adopted; it won because it was the stronger team. It was led by Ernest Erbstein, a sideline genius. A Hungarian Jew, Erbstein had endured Jewish labor camps and owed his life to his team's president, Novo. Torino had its share of off days, when laziness got the best of them. At that point, Oreste Bolmida, the trumpeter fan, would step in to sound the charge. Valentino Mazzola would roll up his sleeves, and his teammates would follow suit. That would spell doom for their opponents. Mazzola and

Loik would lead Torino to five championships in a row, and two Italian cups, with Mazzola becoming top scorer in the 1946–47 season.

BUT, IN THE spring of 1949, winning the *scudetto* was not a foregone conclusion. Inter was four points behind, and the teams had a head-to-head at San Siro. Then there were four games left. If the Nerazzurri won, they would be within two points. A friendly in Lisbon was on the line; the club had arranged for plane tickets and visas to Portugal well in advance, but Novo didn't mince words: lose and you stay in Italy. Inter's front line was fierce. Lorenzi, István Nyers, and Amedeo Amadei were all quick on the draw. And Torino was down Valentino. The match was Milan's to lose.

Inter attacked but didn't execute. Scoring on Granata's goalkeeper Valerio Bacigalupo proved impossible.

The account of Luigi Chierici, founding editor of *Stadio*, helps frame what happened:

> At one point a goal looked all but certain. Amadei threaded a pass to Gino Armano and Armano quickly returned the ball to the center forward. From forty feet out, he struck the ball hard, a waist-high drive at a sharp angle, but Bacigalupo read the play and managed to stop the shot. In the twenty-third minute, Lorenzi appeared destined to score with a deft feint, but just as he was about to pull the trigger, in came Fadini, trapping the ball with his

> foot. The ball stayed put and Lorenzi went flying. Despite a chorus of boos, the referee did not award a foul.

The match ended 0–0. Renato Casalbore again: Every time Inter's attack carved out a route to the goal, Bacigalupo stepped in. The draw with Milan has to be considered a victory for Torino, and if one name stands out, it has to be that of their goalkeeper. I believe Bacigalupo delivered one of the finest performances of his career, certainly his best of the season. Twice he sprang up and denied the strikes of Amadei and Lorenzi when they were inches away from the coveted goal.

RIGHT, AMADEI AND Lorenzi. They had the chance to put the championship back in play, to keep Torino from travelling to Portugal, to change the course of history. It would have taken only a touch more accuracy, a bounce off the goal-post, a different tilt of the pitch, or simply a less superhuman Bacigalupo.

But Torino packed its bags. As did Casalbore, having been invited to cover Lisbon with three other journalists, including Renato Tosatti and Luigi Cavallero. The fourth and most famous of them had to cancel. Nicolò Carosio, the first radio sports commentator, would have gladly boarded the plane, but the friendly against Benfica coincided with his son's confirmation. It was family over football, at least this once.

Meanwhile, journalists continued to talk about the draw

against Inter. Ciro Verratti wrote in the *Corriere della Sera*: "The final hope was shattered. Despite hammering away, Inter failed to break through Granata's defense, allowing Torino to sew another scudetto onto the jerseys of the champions." He goes on, in what, in retrospect, is a chilling aside: "The championship is dead. We might as well lay it to rest. So said one diehard Nerazzurri fan at the end of the match, and perhaps the gentleman didn't realize that all that had died was the dream of Inter. And if anything, it was that castle in the air that deserved to be given a funeral." Death, funerals: a few days later those words would be on the lips of millions of Italians, but they'd no longer be well-worn metaphors.

The whole team was on board the Lisbon-bound Fiat G.212 three-engine airliner that took off on May 1. Even the feverish Mazzola and the run-down Virgilio Maroso. Aldo Ballarin requested that his brother Dino, the third goalkeeper, be included in the lineup, and his wish was granted. Renato Gandolfi, Bacigalupo's understudy, remained in Turin, much to his disappointment (at least at the time). The long-injured substitute Sauro Tomà also stayed home. They made a technical stop in Barcelona and had lunch at the airport with AC Milan, who were on their way to Madrid for a friendly against Real Madrid. Over wine and steak, someone proposed that the two teams square off in Barcelona, at Espanyol's stadium. AC Milan's manager, Antonio Busini, tried to convince Torino's general manager, Rinaldo Agnisetta. It would simply have meant delaying their return flight. No big deal, if there hadn't been the last four league games still to be played. Of course, they had a narrow window of time and the *scudetto* hadn't technically been clinched yet. Agnisetta mulled it over, maybe consulted with Novo over the phone. The final answer was no. It was another pivotal moment in history. If only Torino had agreed . . .

Lisbon felt more like vacation than work. On Monday they went shopping, mostly for wine and spirits. Later that evening there was an official dinner given by the mayor. Neither side spoke the other's language but understanding one another wasn't a problem. Tuesday, May 3, was match day. Torino took pains not to spoil the celebration for captain Ferreira, and Portugal's Benfica won 4–3 before a crowd of forty thousand—plus one: Umberto di Savoia, the former king of Italy living in exile in nearby Cascais. The postcard moment came at the final whistle when the two captains embraced.

Thank you, Valentino, from the bottom of my heart.

It was a pleasure and an honor, Francisco.

That evening the Italians and Portuguese dined together. They drank, they sang, they danced. At midnight, the Torino men thanked their hosts and said their goodbyes. Their return flight was scheduled for 9:40 a.m. the next day, Wednesday, May 4. With another stopover in Barcelona. They had a long day ahead of them.

On the morning Torino bid farewell to Lisbon, the sun was shining. But there were reports of rain and fog in Italy, especially around Turin. In 1974, Novo's right-hand man, Roberto Copernico, recalled those hours in an interview with Guido Magni for *La Gazzetta dello Sport*: "The president was bedridden, with a vexing case of bronchitis. I had to cancel my trip, too. I was on the national teams committee and had to be in Genoa for a second division selection match. The team was supposed to land in Milan. Our bus, the legendary Conte Rosso, had left for Malpensa late in the morning. That afternoon I was at Novo's house. Around 4:00 p.m. the sky turned dark. And a hard, fall-like rain came down."

Foregoing Milan, the G.212 eventually set its course for Turin. We'll never know the real reason for the change of plans. The plane made its last contact with the control tower at 5:00 p.m., to communicate the weather: wind gusts, showers, and clouds 500 meters above the city. The commander of the aircraft, Pierluigi Meroni, reported that he was proceeding at an altitude of 2,000 meters. Or so his altimeter told him. But that was incorrect. The plane was flying much lower. At 5:05 p.m. the G.212 airliner crashed into the retaining wall of the Basilica of Superga, which sits 672 meters above sea level. After that, silence—a silence only broken by the falling rain and the spitting flames.

As Copernico had it,

> At 5:20 p.m. Secretary Giusti reported that a plane had crashed at Superga. Novo and I weren't worried. We were convinced that our plane was landing in Milan. As the minutes passed, doubt crept in. I got into my car and headed for Superga. Gradually our doubt gave way to certainty. In the square of

> the basilica a small crowd had gathered. I was met by Dr. Allitto, head of Turin's rapid response team. He embraced me, shouting, "Copernico! Copernico!" The horrible truth of it hit me. "All of them?" I asked. "Yes, all of them," he replied. I fainted. They took me back to the city. I had to break the news to Novo. The president was still completely in the dark. I tried to stall, but he knew from the way I carried myself, from the look on my face. It was as if he'd lost all his children in one fell swoop.

For a few minutes, a rumor went around that put hope in people's hearts. Not everyone was on the plane: Valentino Mazzola, having not fully recovered, had decided to stay an extra day in Lisbon.

Sadly, it wasn't true.

At 7:00 p.m., just shy of two hours after the disaster, the writer Dino Buzzati left his office at the *Corriere della Sera*. By 9:00 p.m. he had arrived at Superga. His is the most famous account of the incident:

> It was still raining. Low clouds quivered above the illuminated city. Water, mud, deserted streets. Until a dark motionless group appeared, standing in front of a low, long wall. It was the cemetery wall, and the group consisted of relatives and friends waiting expectantly. Then came the

> motorcade. What was left of the thirty-one dead. Who could believe that all that human life, youth, muscles, the rush of the sport and roar of the crowd and victories, all that romance now lay, by some atrocious spell, behind the tinted windows of those six or seven cars cutting across the lonely outskirts of the city in the rain? Without warning those wizards of the pitch, those athletes whom little boys from the suburbs dream of becoming during their mud-bound matches, were nothing but men, young creatures with trophies who, with the passage of time, will gradually fade away.

Indro Montanelli, a journalist from Fucecchio, stayed in Milan and penned a story worthy of his legendary status. "Today," he wrote in the *Corriere*,

> looking out the window, I didn't see the little boys playing soccer in St. Mark's Square. I know them by the names they've given themselves. "Mazzola" is a stocky boy with blonde hair and a wide, beaming face. The slender, nervous, dark-haired "Gabetto" never fails to tease his hair even when the match is at its most animated. "Bacigalupo" usually defends the goal and is surprisingly agile for a boy of his build.... They practice for their big Sunday match, when the crowd of passersby also gathers to watch. During one showdown, the boy known as "Grezar"

> was stripped of his adopted name by his teammates, right there on the pitch, and given another, more modest moniker. Today his sense of diminishment was felt by all.... Every little boy in Saint Mark's was now stuck with his ordinary name. Mazzola was just Mario Dubini, a fourth grader. It fell to him to read the paper to his classmates who had gathered in a semicircle around him. Now and then he would brush a lock of hair that fell from his forehead and take the opportunity to furtively wipe away his tears.

Montanelli also made a suggestion. And although it would remain a suggestion, it testifies to the shock felt throughout the country.

> If the May 22 match against Austria is to be played, then my colleague Carosio, who escaped the disaster by a miracle, should make a special broadcast for the children of Italy. He should name the substitute players after the departed. "Mazzola passes to Menti, Menti back to Castigliano," he should say into the microphone. That way at least the children aren't deprived of the illusion of immortality. It is barely five days since we last saw them play here in Milan. And tomorrow the grass will already be growing over the graves of those eighteen young athletes who seemed to symbolize

> a Homeric, eternal, miraculous youth. How can the boys in St. Mark's Square and all across Italy comprehend that? In the eyes of those who believe in them, heroes have always been immortal. This way the children will believe that Torino isn't dead; it's just on the road.

When we last saw AC Milan, they were at the airport in Barcelona, having lunch with their colleagues from Torino, and entertaining the idea—which would be immediately shelved—to play a friendly on Spanish soil. Afterward the team took the field against Real, on May 4, at around the same time the Granata plane crashed into the basilica. They didn't learn of the tragedy until after the match. President Umberto Trabattoni immediately changed the team's itinerary: they would return to Milan by train. The journey lasted two days and was made more somber by the thought of those who were gone and the regret for not having staged that friendly match that would have saved the life of Mazzola and his teammates.

May 6 was the day of the funeral. Thirty-one coffins were lined up: eighteen players followed by the coaches, with Erbstein at the head, plus managers, journalists, and crew members. A huge crowd attended: as many as six hundred thousand. In a column in *La Gazzetta del Popolo*, Marziano Bernardi wrote:

> They say you can no longer find a flower in Turin. It's true. Every last one in the city is there, its petals

> strewn to mark the route of the funeral procession. Roses, carnations, and pansies rained down from balconies and loggias, from the tall pedestals of monuments, from cornices and rooftops, to cover the thirty-one coffins that already bore wreaths. Turin was one big flower. In an hour of intense mourning the city gave back what it had had, with the gentle outpouring of its stirred soul.

The city wasn't the only one in mourning. There were the colleagues of the eighteen players who died at Superga, some of whom remained inconsolable. Amedeo Amadei, for one. He carried with him the regret for those unconverted goals during the Inter–Torino match on April 30. It was a regret that would haunt him for the rest of his life and that Roberto Copernico reflected on in his 1974 interview in *La Gazzetta dello Sport*:

> I remember a story that Amadei later told me. In a run down the wing he found himself facing Bacigalupo, who dove at his feet. He didn't hesitate to leap over Torino's goalkeeper. It was a charitable move: it would have been an easy goal, but it would also have meant slamming into his opponent. At the funeral, in tears, Amadei said, "If I had kicked him, I would have scored. I'd have sent Bacigalupo to the hospital, but I would have saved them all."

The same thought troubled Benito Lorenzi for the rest of his life: How did I not foresee the goalkeeper leaving the goal? Why did that shot end up across the goal line and not in the goal? Couldn't my teammates have set me up better? Night after night "Veleno" awoke from a nightmare: "Of all days Bacigalupo had to play the perfect game that day. All it would have taken was a moment's hesitation, even the slightest. No one would have blamed him for losing after all the saves he'd made. And I would have played God knows how many games alongside my friend Valentino, with the nationals, maybe even with Inter."

Regret, remorse. But at a certain point Benito Lorenzi stopped grieving and focused all his attention on Mazzola's sons, Sandro and Ferruccio. He knew he had a debt to pay. He'd become a kind of second father to them, shuttling them in his car to the stadium. Sandro was especially promising, so Lorenzi took the time to teach him the tricks of the trade.

Every soccer fan knows how the story ends: fifteen years after the Superga disaster, Inter would win its first Champions Cup by beating Real Madrid in the final. Sandro Mazzola would score two goals and at the end of the match the great Ferenc Puskás would whisper a kind of incantation in his ear: "I played with your father and let me tell you, you're worthy of him." That may have been the moment Benito Lorenzi cleared his conscience.

POSTSCRIPT: AN INTERVIEW WITH SANDRO MAZZOLA

MAY 2023

Buongiorno, Sandro Mazzola. Tell us, what do you remember about Benito Lorenzi?

Lorenzi adored my father. He carried it around inside him. He used to come collect my brother, Ferruccio, and me and drive us to Superga or to the cemetery to visit my father's grave. Then he would take us to see Inter. His love for people, for the fans, was boundless. Soccer was everything to him.

How did he and your father become friends?

I think it started when they played together on the national team. Members of Torino were regularly called up. Eight or nine of them played. Others were called up but never took the field. Traditionally, players and coaching staff would go on a walk together on the eve of each match. The coaches would go through the names of each player who would take the field, one by one. There must have come a day when my father told Ferruccio Novo and the others, "Look, this guy is good, why don't you let him play?" He was talking about Lorenzi. Lorenzi, who was your typical, hot-blooded, curious Tuscan, had positioned himself behind my father so he could hear the conversation. From then on that was it: my dad became a god to him. And Lorenzi did in fact play that match, though I don't remember which it was.

Is it true that Lorenzi was actively trying to bring your father to Inter?

I've heard that. I never talked to Benito about it, so I have no actual memories of that. But I think there might have been some truth to it. My father was the kind of person who, once he sets his mind to something, does everything in his power to achieve it.

Did you ever talk to Lorenzi about that Inter vs. Torino match?

No. I was still a child when the Superga disaster happened. And even after that he probably didn't want to reopen old wounds. But I did know that Ferruccio Novo promised my father he would only allow them to play Lisbon if Torino didn't lose to Inter. And I know about the chances that Lorenzi had to score a winning goal that would probably have changed the course of history.

What did Benito Lorenzi become for you after May 4?

In a way, for my brother and me, he took the place of our dad. He was the one who would pick us up at home or take us out to the field or for a walk. He became a central, indispensable figure. Maybe it had to do with his remorse for not scoring in that Inter–Torino match. Who knows? He never told me that. He often spoke about matches and goals, but never about that particular match.

Lorenzi was certainly no saint on the field.

True! But on the other hand, given his style of play, he was bound to take a hit now and then. So instead of turning the other cheek, he tried to strike back.

In the end, he was the one who brought you to Inter.

Yes, he was the one. I had a stepfather, and he wanted to bring me. Then one day, Benito took me by the hand and said: "Ok, you come with me. I'll take you to watch them train." He was the one who took charge. At that point it was impossible to say no to him. So one fine day I found myself on the pitch for tryouts.

Underneath it all, Benito Lorenzi was a good guy . . .

You can say that again. At least from what I saw. I don't know if he had another side that he preferred to keep hidden. But on the pitch, it was best to steer clear of him. If someone talked trash to him, sooner or later he would retaliate. He might wait for a goal kick to get his revenge, when everyone is huddled close and it's hard to determine who did what to whom.

Did he often talk to you about Valentino?

Sure. In my opinion, he wanted us to remember him as a parent who had died too soon. Frequent trips to Superga served to keep his memory alive. For Benito, my father was simply the best there was. Sometimes, when my brother Ferruccio and I went on a walk with him, he would be silent for a while and then suddenly launch into a story about a game, an episode. You see, he'd say, on such and such a day your father did this, your father did that. And we would listen in awe, as if that goal, or that play, were happening before our very eyes.

СССР

CHAPTER 5

A MONDAY GOAL: SPAIN UNDER FRANCO, THE EASTERN BLOC, AND A DIVIDED EUROPE

MATCH
Soviet Union vs. Yugoslavia

FINAL SCORE
2–1

WHEN
July 10, 1960

WHERE
Parc des Princes, Paris

TRACKING HIM DOWN wasn't easy, but in the end I managed. There he stood, his gray hair close-cropped, wearing a black-and-white checkered jacket and a pair of dark glasses that most likely masked a problem with his eyesight: Viktor Vladimirovich Ponedelnik. We were in RAI's Moscow correspondence office, just a few weeks away from the 2004 European Championship finals. And it was about that championship that I wanted to talk with him, specifically about the first tournament held in 1960. Ponedelnik had scored the winning goal in the final between the Soviet

Union and Yugoslavia. It was a 120-minute-long match. "I made the day of whoever was writing the headlines in my country," he told me with a half smile. He had a point. In Russian, *ponedelnik* means Monday, and the final began on Sunday, July 10, at 8:00 p.m. in France. Ponedelnik scored his goal at the stroke of midnight in his home country. The pun practically wrote itself: "Monday converts on Monday."

Of all the players who determined the outcome of a European Championship final, Ponedelnik is the least known. There is no comparison between him and his contemporaries, like Gigi Riva or Gerd Müller or Antonin Panenka; not to mention players who succeeded him, from Michel Platini to Marco van Basten. I confess that, before I flew to Moscow to interview him, I didn't even know what he looked like. Only a few photos of him exist, all of them dated, along with a tiny amount of low-quality film footage. A lot, I think, depended on the fact that the first continental tournament had been met with broad indifference—besides, perhaps, by the countries involved. Moreover, Europe had gotten its act together very late, at least compared to *the other continent* leading the soccer charge. In fact, the first Copa America, the South American counterpart to Europe's final, began all the way back in 1916. In short, while Europeans were dying in the trenches of the First World War, South Americans were playing soccer at the highest level.

It took the arrival of Henri Delaunay, the UEFA (Union of European Football Associations) executive who most believed in the project. Not that he found a receptive audience—on the contrary. For many insiders at the time, a continental tournament seemed more like an inconvenience to slot between World Cups. West German coach Sepp Herberger, for one, said as much. And as late as 1957, legendary FIFA president Jules Rimet pronounced roughly the following in a speech at a UEFA convention: "Do we really want soccer in our countries to be all about competitions? We put too much emphasis on the competitive side of the game and risk overcommercializing the sport." Too many matches, too much concern about money: that was the gist. I wonder what Monsieur Rimet would say about soccer today, when games are played eleven months of the year, and the most lauded players take the field no fewer than sixty times a year.

IN THE END, however, the European tourney was arranged. Seventeen federations answered the call. Seventeen out of the thirty-three teams that were registered with the UEFA at that time. No England, no Germany, no Italy. Since the war, the Italian national team had been entrusted to nine different technical commissions, and each successive commission had barely been an improvement over the last. The truth is that what it lacked most were the raw goods. Ever since Superga, Italy had been able to count on only one talent that has lived up to the tradition: Giampiero Boniperti. That's not enough to think big. After their disastrous loss (0–3) to Puskás's Hungary, in the first ever match at Rome's Stadio Olimpico, a radical decision was made to bar foreigners, to close the borders, to make space for youth clubs, known as farm teams. Nor would the national play in the European tournament.

The measure to seal the borders is often attributed to Giulio Andreotti, then undersecretary to the presidency of the council. I interviewed him in Merano immediately after my meeting with Ponedelnik, and he offered this reconstruction of events: “The proposal wasn’t mine. It was the federation’s. President Ottorino Barassi begged the government to adopt a measure concerning visas, employment, and residence. It became known as the ‘Andreotti Veto,’ but in reality I was merely carrying out someone else’s wishes. That said, the measure did have its admirers because in some ways it promoted feeder teams.”

And this is how Giampiero Boniperti, also in 2004, answered my question as to whether refusing to play in the first European Championship had been the right choice:

> I don’t think so. Even when you perform poorly, you still learn something. You improve, in life and not just in soccer. I understand that Italians followed the national team more than any other, that it was the team whose performances caused collective mood swings. Every defeat was a tragedy, and in those years it lost a lot. I remember the great administrator Artemio Franchi wanted to restrict their play to a minimum because the national team was the team that created the most fodder for the

> papers, that set the tone for all Italian sports. But I would have played. For me, getting out on the field was fun.

Soccer and politics. The two worlds have always attracted and repelled one another, and sometimes butted heads. As they did during the first Henri Delaunay Cup, aptly named for the man who had given the most to create a continental tournament for national teams. The seventeen teams became sixteen after Czechoslovakia eliminated the Republic of Ireland in the first round. The format was simple: rounds of sixteen and quarterfinals with home and away games, then semifinals and single-match finals.

THE TURNING POINT came in the quarterfinals: the scoreboard read SPAIN VS. SOVIET UNION. On paper—and bearing in mind the teams not participating—it was the mother of all matches, a preview of the final. Spain had Alfredo Di Stéfano, the man who had made Real Madrid great but who, for a variety of reasons, had yet to find a national team that could make the most of his immense talent. The Soviet Union had Lev Yashin, the world's best goalkeeper, who chose to play soccer after winning the USSR ice hockey cup and whose massive size made the goal appear tiny.

Di Stéfano vs. Yashin, then. Or at least that's how it should have been—a showdown for discerning palates. Except that Spain vs. the Soviet Union could also be read as a showdown between Francoism and Communism. Politics, again. So, can we really be sure that the (athletic and diplomatic) conditions existed for the double game to be played? It was one of the things I asked Ponedelnik during our long conversation in 2004:

> I remember those days well. In preparation for the quarterfinal with Spain, we played Poland in a friendly at Luzhniki Stadium. It was my first time on the national team. There were 105,000 spectators, among them Spain's coach, Helenio Herrera, and with him the top officials of the federation. We won 7–1 and I scored three goals. We played a great game. As far as I know, once back home the Spanish managers were summoned by Francisco Franco. He asked them if they could guarantee that Spain could beat us. Maybe no one felt like taking the risk, since the fact remains that USSR vs. Spain wasn't played.

Could Ponedelnik really have known all that, especially about the Spanish team? It's a legitimate question, so it makes sense to get the other side's version of events. I asked Luisito Suárez, who at the time was not yet a guiding light for Inter Milan but an anchor for Barcelona and Spain: "The gathering for the first match," he said in 2004, "had been set in Madrid."

> We arrived separately, those from Barcelona and those from Seville, and were summoned to federation headquarters. The mood was strange. We were told that we would have to wait for the green light from Franco or at least the minister for sport. The mood was eerie. At one point the FIFA president entered the room where the politicians had gathered. And we were left outside waiting. The wait was interminable. As the minutes passed, pessimism came over me and my teammates. Our hunch soon gave way to certainty. Finally, we were told that the game would not be played because there were no diplomatic relations between the two countries.

Suárez was telling the truth. Things had stood that way since the Spanish Civil War, when the Soviet Union had supported the Republicans over Franco's Falangists.

The Spanish dictator had the last word: he would never let his country's team play on Communist soil. In short, politics trumped sports, just as it had two years earlier, when the caudillo forbade Real Madrid from flying to Latvia, then a Soviet republic, to face ASK Riga in the semifinals of the newly formed European basketball championship. The only difference was that, this time, they were national teams, not clubs. The players, at least the Spanish players, resented the decision, but back then you couldn't say as much in public. In extremis, they suggested to Madrid that there be a single match played on neutral territory, but the proposal was rejected. The Soviets weren't stupid: at a single stroke they would advance a round and get rid of one of its most competitive opponents.

But all those many years later, Ponedelnik also expressed regret: "It was unfortunate. There were many Spaniards living here among us who had fled during the Civil War. Their children were born and raised in the Soviet Union. We would have liked to play for them, too, as well as for the chance to play against the many outstanding players who wore Spain's jersey."

AT THIS POINT we should clear up one matter of curiosity. What's with Ponedelnik's name? Why Monday? For that story, we have to travel back to 1861, when Tsar Alexander II ordered the abolition of serfdom, a measure that directly affected the ancestors of the Soviet center forward. Bureaucracy dictated that the names of the former serfs be entered into special registers. According to family lore, one clerk on duty, perhaps having had too many glasses of vodka, allegedly got mixed up and transcribed the day of the week in the column designated for surnames. And what day was it? You guessed it: Monday.

That the last stage of the first European national team competition should be held in France was practically a matter of course. Henri Delaunay, who passed away in 1955, when the tournament still only existed in his and a few other visionaries' minds, was French. Besides, France was the only country to have presented itself as a candidate. True, Spain had also made a bid, but things turned out the way they turned out. In France, four days of matches were scheduled, from July 6 to 10, and two cities chosen to host them, Marseille and Paris. Alongside France and the Soviet Union were Yugoslavia and Czechoslovakia.

What immediately leaps out is the overwhelming presence of Eastern Europe, the part of the continent that most believed in the European competition, perhaps to spread propaganda. It is striking to read the names today: the Soviet Union, Yugoslavia, and Czechoslovakia—nations no longer found on the map, each having been swept away, a few years apart, by the fits and starts of history.

The tournament odds favored France, which in addition to playing at home had come in third place at the Swedish World Cup two years earlier; however, their three strongest players—Just Fontaine, Raymond Kopa, and Roger Piantoni—were sidelined due to injuries. Indeed, la France lost in the semifinals to Yugoslavia, which, once it could align its Serbian, Croatian, and Bosnian sides, would later reward us with moments of sublime soccer.

IN THE EYES of the host country, the match was more athletic suicide than defeat. France was at the Parc des Princes and lead 3–1, then 4–2. With just a quarter of an hour to go, it looked like it was all over. But then the Slavs scored three goals in four minutes and secured a place in the final. At the Vélodrome in Marseille, on the other hand, all went as expected in the match between the Soviet Union and Czechoslovakia: the Sbornaya (Russia's national team) won handily, with two goals by Valentin Ivanov and the final boot by Victor "Monday" to finish 3–0.

It was only Ponedelnik's third appearance in a national tournament, and in truth he should not have been at the center of the attack. The best—in that and other roles—was another player, also born in 1937, named Eduard Streltsov, whom some have gone so far as to call "the white Pelé." But he had spent the last few years in a Siberian gulag on an alleged sexual assault charge that he would forever deny having committed and that would cost him a big chunk of his career. With Streltsov out, it was open terrain for Ponedelnik. Even if he played for Rostov, a team from the city of the same name on the Don River located six hundred miles from Moscow. That was no small matter, on paper: in Soviet soccer, the clubs from the capital are the ones that count.

The kid knew he was the designated starter, partly because there were no alternatives, but he had a serious liability: he suffered from sudden asthma attacks. In the national team's training camp just outside Moscow, a room was set up especially for him. There, doctors would treat him when his breathing began to fail. Twenty years earlier, some sources say, Nazi general Friedrich Paulus, who commanded at the Battle of Stalingrad that sealed the fate of the Second World War, was held prisoner in the same room. From time to time, some of Ponedelnik's teammates jokingly referred to him as "Paulus."

Fortunately, his asthma didn't act up that July 10, 1960, at the Parc des Princes stadium. The Soviet Union's center forward was in terrific form, and even the adverse weather didn't faze him. "It was cold and very damp. At one point it started to rain. It was more than just a game. Once again politics impacted soccer. In those years relations between Tito and Khrushchev were tense. They were both Communists, but different in kind. Yugoslavia wanted to win at all costs, by any means, because those were the orders from Belgrade. It made for a jittery match. The stadium was half empty but after being evenly split the few Frenchmen there decided to support our team."

After his soccer career ended, Ponedelnik turned for a time to journalism. When I ask him about the final, his account sounds a lot like the reporting that journalists used to dictate over the phone for the next day's paper. "It was an evenly split match until our opponents took the lead at the end of the first half thanks to Milan Galić. His sensational strike was the only way to get past Yashin. The real force to be reckoned with was Dragoslav Šekularac. The midfielder was the full package, a combination of technique and vision. This was the same guy whom the Brazilians invited to teach in their soccer schools. Can you imagine? A Yugoslavian teaching soccer in Brazil?"

Ponedelnik remembers everything about that final:

With just enough time to put the ball back in play
the referee blows the whistle. The first half ends

> and we go back to the locker room. Our coach Kachalin comes up to each of us and tells us what we have to do to turn the game around. It was your typical coach spiel. But the most powerful words were spoken by the team trainer Andrey Starostin. He told us that we hadn't shown what we were made of during the first half and that our real strengths were still a mystery to our opponents. And then, to incentivize us, he added that an entire country was staying up to hear the news from Paris. We couldn't let all those people down.

Starostin's speech was just the jolt the players needed. The equalizer arrived in the opening minutes of the second half. A long-range shot from Valentin Bubukin bounced off goalkeeper Blagoje Vidinić and with a tap from close-range Slava Metreveli put the ball in the back of the net. Ponedelnik again: "We were never scared we'd lose. We'd grown up at the turn of the Second World War with the spirit of winners. We embodied a soccer that was played in the streets and courtyards. Hours and hours of pure football, even skipping school. That gave us a winning mentality. We were bullish. We never gave up. We knew that the final in Paris would be the game of a lifetime."

But their opponents showed up to play, too. From then on, Yugoslavia stopped making defensive mistakes, and the match went into overtime. "After the ninetieth minute we sat on the field. The grass was wet. It was cold but we didn't mind. I remember someone lying down and closing his eyes as if to concentrate. No one thought for a second we might lose. And then we had noticed that by the end of the second half something was going on with Yugoslavia's ranks. They'd made many mistakes, the players were pointing the finger at one another. It signaled to us that their team play was gone."

Meanwhile the clock was racing toward 10:00 p.m. Paris time. Midnight in Moscow. In the center of the Soviet Union, Sunday was starting to give way to Monday. As Ponedelnik explains it:

> The coincidence didn't occur to me. My mind was entirely on the match. The score hadn't budged, in all likelihood we'd replay the final two days later. Then, with seven minutes to go, Mikheil Meshki carries the ball up left field. There are two of us in the area, me and Ivanov. He was a really smart player, and led two opponents away, so that I found myself unguarded. I signal to Meshki to cross. The ball comes right to me. It's just a matter of choosing when to head the ball, one of my specialties. I can't even see the trajectory. I could tell by the screams from the stands that something must have happened. A mass of muddy bodies knocks me onto the grass. It's my teammates hugging me. I realize that I've scored, that we're ahead, that we're a step away from winning.

What Ponedelnik couldn't know was the explosive reaction in Moscow. They wouldn't tell him until the next day:

> They didn't have TV in the Soviet Union to broadcast the game. People had to tune in to the radio. Nikolai Ozerov, a legend, was doing the commentary. When I scored, he started shouting. "He scored on Monday! He scored on Monday!" I don't know how many times he said it. All the papers would pick up the pun. We were the first European champions. Thanks to me. I can never forget the victory lap at the Parc des Princes, passing the cup from hand to hand. Later our families told us that the whole country had been awake, glued to their radios. There wasn't a window in Moscow that wasn't lit up. In the end, people poured into the streets to celebrate. It was an unprecedented sight for a soccer match.

The players would take a second victory lap with the cup once they returned home. "From the Moscow airport," says Ponedelnik, "they took us straight to Luzhniki Stadium, each of us in a car with the top down. We wore our track-suits emblazoned with the letters CCCP. People had packed into the stands, as if that day were the final. But it was just in honor of us players." As he spoke, Viktor Monday's voice cracked. Too bad he's got on those dark glasses, I thought to myself. I'll never know whether, remembering that time, the hero of Paris was moved to tears.

THERE IS ONE more episode between the final at Parc des Princes and the catwalk in Moscow that's worth repeating, one more tile left to complete the mosaic. In the aftermath of their victory over Yugoslavia, the team was still in Paris. The program included a gala dinner at the restaurant in the Eiffel Tower. The night before, the players had tossed back a few beers near their hotel and only gotten a few hours of sleep. They were keen to return home. At one point, all eyes turned to a distinguished gentleman, wearing a hat and chewing a cigar, who was making the rounds. In disbelief, the players started elbowing each other.

"Is that?"

"You think it's him?"

"It can't be."

But it was. Santiago Bernabéu, under whose presidency Real Madrid had won five consecutive champions cups, the most recent just a few weeks before the European nationals. What was Bernabéu doing at the Eiffel Tower? After all, Spain hadn't won the title.

The new champions were eager to know, and it only took a minute to satisfy their curiosity. Bernabéu had something in his pocket and pulled it out. It was a checkbook. He had climbed all the way to the top of the tower to do business! His

Real Madrid had reached the end of an unrepeatable cycle. Alfredo Di Stéfano was about to turn thirty-four, Ferenc Puskás was just a year younger. He had to begin thinking about replacements. And who better than the boys who had just put on that show, beating first Czechoslovakia and then Yugoslavia?

"With the help of an interpreter he approached me and some of my teammates," said Ponedelnik. "Yashin, Igor Netto, Metreveli, Ivanov. He said he wanted us for Real Madrid. And he added that we were free to set our asking price."

Perhaps we ought to be wary of Ponedelnik's story: transplanting five Soviet players in one stroke to a club like Real Madrid, then the most prominent team in Franco's Spain, seems a bit rich, especially at that time in history. Santiago Bernabéu did indeed climb the Eiffel Tower, but he came down still bearing his burden of dreams—and dreams they would remain.

> It didn't take long for our managers to figure out what was going on. They ran over and told the interpreter to inform Bernabéu that we were all under contract and couldn't accept. But where was our contract? It was a lie, obviously. In Soviet Union soccer there were no contracts, there was no such thing as professionalism as we know it today. It wasn't the first time that market agents were hovering over us, ready to make princely offers,

> to the point that during away games, whether it was the club or the national team, we were always accompanied by someone from the KGB. We were never left alone, especially when we happened to be walking down the street or entering a bar, a store. Just talking about certain things scared us.

The dream of Spain fizzled. Viktor Ponedelnik would remain at Rostov, and Santiago Bernabéu would ask Di Stéfano and Puskás to tough it out another few years. How much did the European champions earn for the title in Paris? I'll tell you how much: the equivalent of two hundred dollars each. There is talk of legendary gifts—cars, apartments, sundry perks—but for the most part these are pure invention. According to one such rumor, Nikita Khrushchev himself gave the author of the winning goal a luxury car. Viktor Ponedelnik has been asked about it ten, one hundred, a thousand times over the years. His back-and-forth with the periodical *Sport-Express* in 1995 is worth remembering:

"Is the story about being given the car true?"

"It is, it is. I'm just waiting for the gift to arrive."

CHAPTER 6

THE HUNDRED-HOUR WAR:
THE 1960S AND LATIN AMERICA'S POLITICAL MOSAIC

MATCH
El Salvador vs. Honduras

FINAL SCORE
3–2

WHEN
June 27, 1969

WHERE
Estadio Azteca, Mexico City

THE HONDURAN RADIO broadcaster announced that Apollo 11 had launched from Cape Kennedy. Three astronauts—Armstrong, Collins, Aldrin—were headed to the moon. Man was getting closer to the stars, discovering new worlds, penetrating the vast stretches of the galaxy. From every corner of Earth congratulations were pouring into Houston. Mankind was celebrating that triumph of reason and exactitude.

These words emerged from the typewriter of Ryszard Kapuściński, one of the greatest war reporters of all time. They mark the beginning of a mission whose high point came on July 20, 1969, with Neil Armstrong, the first man to step on lunar soil, uttering a phrase that billions of people now know by heart: "That's one small step for man, one giant leap for mankind." Anyone over the age of sixty-five remembers where they were while history was being made. For Italians, that night we were split between Tito Stagno and Ruggero Orlando, who were arguing on air, one from Rome and the other from Houston. "He touched down!" "No, he didn't!"

In his correspondences, Kapuściński has neither the time nor the inclination to elaborate on the matter. He makes passing reference to it, a handful of lines while in Honduras doing what he does best: reporting on war and its aftermath. He's been through this before, but the conflict is different this time, in large part because it was over and done in the span of four days, from July 14 to 18. He gave it a name, too, one that would circle the globe, a phrase worthy of copyright: the first "soccer war." That's right; this time it was over soccer. Over a ball that rolled on a green rectangle and somehow triggered a conflict that in a hundred hours would leave six thousand people dead.

The teams were Honduras and El Salvador. What was meant to be two matches went into a third tiebreaker. It was a showdown between neighboring countries, a derby, the Latin American equivalent of Italy–France or Belgium–Holland. The prize was a spot in the following year's World Cup. The tournament would be played in Mexico. The home team automatically qualified, leaving one slot for another representative from Central and North America. We've come to the semifinals, United States vs. Haiti and, yes, Honduras vs. El Salvador.

SOCCER, IN LATIN America and beyond, is one of many pieces in an extremely complex puzzle where economics and politics play a factor. El Salvador has been independent since 1838. It's a small country, especially compared to others in the region. It has no access to the Atlantic and, on its other side, the coastal strip on the Pacific, it must contend with Honduras's sovereignty over the Gulf of Fonseca. That's no small matter: Fonseca is a crucial hub for trade between North and South America.

In short, El Salvador feels suffocated. And then there's the role of the United States, which is accustomed to doing as it pleases in the backyards of its Central American neighbors, especially then, during the Cold War years, when the Soviet Union represented enemy number one. On December 13, 1960, with the blessing of Washington and newly elected president John Fitzgerald Kennedy, the Central American Common Market, or CACM, was founded, which Honduras, El Salvador, Guatemala, Nicaragua, and, after 1962, Costa Rica belonged to. The region basically relied on one crop: bananas. Millions of bananas were produced and exported, with limited labor costs. For other countries, the United States included, it was far cheaper to import bananas than to grow them. It was a business in the hands of powerful, starred-and-striped multinational corporations (one in particular, the United Fruit Company) and a few local landowning families.

It amounted to a "little game" that basically benefitted everyone: the US government, the production companies, and the Common Market member states, which somehow foresaw themselves escaping the chronic agricultural backwardness in which they were mired. Not everyone benefitted equally, however. Investors preferred those areas where there is already a semblance of technological development, and in that regard El Salvador proved to be the more advanced country, Honduras the more backward. Even in the context of relative poverty, Salvadorans experienced substantial economic growth, which brought with it a decline in infant mortality and an increase in birth rates. Within a short time, the population grew to 3.7 million, as compared to 2.6 in Honduras, though the latter was six times larger than El Salvador.

Exponential population growth in a small territory led to rising unemployment rates. So, to avoid economic collapse and the inevitable popular uprisings that would follow, El Salvador looked to its neighbors in Tegucigalpa. They weren't faring so well themselves, but at least they had large swathes of uncultivated land. Thus, a bilateral immigration treaty was signed in 1967 that created a faster track for citizens of El Salvador, who chose to pack up their belongings and move to Honduras in the hopes of finding freedom of transit, residency opportunities, and the right to work.

In the end, about three hundred thousand people crossed the border. But in doing so they took space and job opportunities away from those born and raised in Honduras. In no time, the situation turned inside out. It was the locals who first complained of unsustainable living conditions, which didn't escape the notice of Honduras's dictator Oswaldo López Arellano, a man backed by landowners with the blessing of the United States. In the spring of 1969, through the National Agrarian Institute, Arellano issued a measure to confiscate land and expel from the country anyone not born in Honduras. For the three hundred thousand in question, it was the end of a dream. They returned home, but home was no guarantee of a job or a portion of land to cultivate or a roof over one's head.

IT WAS ENOUGH to set the two countries down a very dangerous slope. And in 1969, soccer got caught up in the fallout. The schedule for the World Cup qualifying tournament involves two matches, one home and one away. On Sunday, June 8, the match was played in Tegucigalpa, a week later in San Salvador. It's easy to imagine the mood; soccer became an instrument of retaliation for all that had happened in the preceding weeks. Even the most absent-minded observer could see that neither team harbored the slightest hope of winning the World Cup or even making a decent showing.

Before securing a spot in Mexico, there was another hurdle to overcome, too: the final against the winner of Haiti vs. United States. But no one was thinking about that. At that moment, only one thing mattered: defeating the enemy, and, if possible, humiliating them.

It isn't easy to reconstruct those days. Media coverage of the twofer was limited and spotty. In Europe, the season had just ended with Milan scrambling Ajax, led by a very young Johan Cruyff, in the Champions Cup final. It ended 4–1 in favor of the Rossoneri. Amsterdam would have time to regroup. Summer was coming. World Cup qualifiers are only a matter of interest to a handful of insiders. Besides, we're talking about a showdown between Central American teams. There was the business of tensions between the two countries, but in Europe that news was relegated to the international section, far below the fold.

The first match was played on Sunday, June 8, at the Estadio Nacional in Tegucigalpa. Honduras was favored to win, having reached the semifinals by eliminating Costa Rica, perhaps the most talented national team in the region. According to Mauricio "Pipo" Rodríguez, a striker from El Salvador, "[Honduras] had been preparing for the World Cup qualifiers for two years. We'd been at it for a month and a half." Rodríguez would be interviewed many years later by the German journalist Klaus Ehringfeld, one of the few who took the trouble to wipe off the layers of dust that had accumulated over those dramatic days.

Honduras was also favored thanks to its center forward, José Enrique Cardona, who for five years had been racking up points for Atlético Madrid, a club vying for the top spot on the Old Continent. In Spain, Cardona had come away with a championship and a national cup, with the added thrill of scoring the decisive goal in the final against Real Zaragoza. To opponents and teammates alike, he was an extraterrestrial.

The El Salvador team reached its hotel the night before the match. No one had any illusions about being greeted by a welcoming committee with girls in local costumes or flowers or an assortment of tributes. What they found, however, beggars belief. A night of hell ensued: firecrackers, shattered glass, insulting chants, and a procession of automobiles out their window, accompanied by a concert of car horns. There wasn't a moment's peace.

If the goal was to keep the players up all night, that mission was clearly accomplished. "They called us thieves," said Rodríguez. "At first we didn't understand what or who they were referring to. Then it slowly dawned on us that their hatred went beyond soccer." At about the same time, the town was being carpeted with flyers labeling Salvadorans thieves, drunks, and crooks, as well as issuing a warning: "Go home or you'll regret it!" In addition, there was a not-so-subtle reference to farmers and the land allocated and then confiscated by the government in Tegucigalpa.

One could say that the match was ugly and dirty, but

they couldn't claim it was ruthless. Neither side personally insulted anyone, nor were there any hard fouls. The players did what they could, the eighteen thousand people in the stands watched a modest contest unfold, with only one goal, by the Hondurans, scored in the second to last minute by defender Leonard Welch. Whether the final score was 1–0 or 4–0 didn't matter, according to the rules of the qualifiers. If El Salvador won the second match, no matter by how many goals, they'd have to find a neutral stadium for the tiebreaker.

It's never nice to lose right before the referee blows the whistle, but the reaction of Amelia Bolaños that day is hard to fathom. The eighteen-year-old girl from San Salvador was watching the match on TV. When she saw Welch's goal, she lost it; she ran to her father's room, pulled a gun from his drawer and took her own life. That is, at least, how Ryszard Kapuściński told the story years later, overlooking no detail, beginning with the comment that appeared the next day in the newspaper *El Nacional*: "Young woman can't bear to see her homeland brought to its knees." Kapuściński goes on: "The entire capital attended the televised funeral of Amelia Bolaños. Her coffin, draped with the country's flag, was followed by the president of the Republic and cabinet ministers. Behind the members of government came the eleven players from El Salvador who had been booed and spit on at the Tegucigalpa airport that morning and flown home on a special plane."

WE'LL GET BACK to Kapuściński's retelling of events. A week passed between the away and home games. During that time relations between Honduras and El Salvador became increasingly strained. The expulsion of Salvadoran migrants suddenly accelerated. Enter the men of La Mancha Brava, a paramilitary organization, under the orders of dictator López Arellano, a designated commando who usually "handled" school strikes and, more generally, suppressed protests against the regime (you can imagine by what means). This time they trained their focus on dispossessed farmers who refused to leave their lands. The newspapers—Salvadoran, of course—described families being beaten to a pulp, women being raped, and other horrors.

Honduras's national team decided to leave for San Salvador two days before the match. In a sobering display, military jets escorted the team to the threshold of Honduran airspace. The reception organized at the entrance of the hotel put that of a week earlier to shame, this time with the roles reversed. Dead mice, rotten eggs, and bags of excrement were launched at the players' windows. Plus the customary flares, of course, which only by pure chance missed the players. Not so lucky was the chaperone: a local boy, he would die from injuries sustained in one of the explosions. Forty years later, Marco Antonio Mendoza, a midfielder and future secretary of Honduras's Football Federation, related a shocking detail: "While all this stuff was being flung at our rooms, a policeman with a megaphone shouted at those thugs something along the lines of, 'Do what you want, just don't damage the hotel.' As if to say that if it were up to law enforcement, they could go ahead and kill us, the important thing was to leave the doors and windows intact." At around 3:00 a.m., with no other alternatives, federation officials decided to take the team to the roof. The noise was deafening, the players had no choice but to plug their ears with cotton. Unable to sleep (have you ever seen a bed on a roof?), they played cards and waited for daybreak.

The problem was that there was still one more night before the match, the night between Saturday, June 14, and Sunday, June 15. Changing hotels made no sense, so in the end they opted for a different solution: the players were split into groups of three and housed with Honduran families living in San Salvador. The five thousand fans who traveled from Tegucigalpa to support their team had it much worse. Their buses became target practice for an assault with rocks and Molotov cocktails. For many, that was the end of the journey, but at least they made it back home with their limbs attached. The less fortunate wound up crowding the hospital wards. According to the final toll, there were even two deaths.

And the match? Right, the match. For obvious reasons, Honduras's players showed up without having trained the night before, and with the sole objective of getting home in one piece. After all, given their victory a week earlier, the worst that could happen is that they'd have one more chance. The federation in Tegucigalpa, for their part, asked FIFA to cancel the match and let the first one stand. The answer from Zurich was a hard no. Honduras reached Flor Blanca Stadium escorted by tanks from the army's 1st Armored Division. Along the way, Kapuściński reports, thousands of people brandished the photo of the nation's new hero, Amelia Bolaños.

There was nothing to do but play. But first came the national anthems. Honduras's anthem was drowned out by booing, but that was nothing; the visiting team's flag was torn to shreds and replaced by a tattered, dirty rag hoisted up the flagpole. The match ended the only way it could—with El Salvador winning 3–0, all goals scored in the first half. "Boy, it's a good thing we lost." The postgame sentiment of Coach Mario Griffin perfectly encapsulated the losing team's state of mind. Who knows what would have happened if the outcome had been different? Outside the stadium they waited for tanks. The players boarded and reached the airport, still in their sweat-soaked jerseys and mud-caked shoes. Getting back home was all that mattered.

THEY OF COURSE had to play a third match on a neutral field. It didn't take long to pick a time and place. The match was slated for June 27 at Mexico City's Estadio Azteca, the same facility, with a capacity of one hundred thousand people, that would host the World Cup final a year later, and before that the semifinal, which Italy and West Germany would turn into the "match of the century," earning them a commemorative plaque outside the entrance gates.

One hundred thousand seats for El Salvador vs. Honduras? Ridiculous. A stadium of thirty thousand would have been enough. Or maybe thirty-five thousand—accounting for five thousand police and military personnel in combat gear. Tensions were high, at least in the stands. Two days earlier, in front of the UN Commission on Human Rights, El Salvador accused Honduras of genocide. That was the first setback. The second, the severing of diplomatic relations, came a few hours later. It was only a matter of time before war would break out. Which side would fire the first shot? With the future uncertain, people turned their attention to soccer: there was a playoff to be played. El Salvador twice took the lead and twice lost it, the second time with the help of goalkeeper Gualberto Fernández, who clumsily tripped over the ball, landed on a defender, and allowed the Honduran striker Rigoberto Gomez to place it in the unguarded goal—classic slipping-on-a-banana-peel material. Poor Fernández, who seemed to have developed myopia, was substituted on the spot.

As with the first two matches, the third wasn't really affected by tensions external to football. It was played without giving a thought to what was happening and what might happen between the two countries. The next day, Mexico City's *El Heraldo* wrote, "The players set aside political tensions and initiated a sportsmanly contest." Extra time was needed for a winning team to emerge, and if no one scored, there would have been a rematch. But that eventuality was averted in the 101st minute, when Pipo "the Pipe" Rodríguez eluded his defensive mark Azulejo Bulnes and slid the ball past goalie Jaime Varela. The goal handed El Salvador a pass to the final. But that wasn't all.

After the referee's final whistle, it was like the scene after any upset: elation for the winners, tears for the losers. Only this time something was different. The players knew it. This wasn't just soccer. Military personnel were gathering at the border of El Salvador and Honduras, ready for action. All that was missing was the green light from high command, and it would be war.

CONFLICT ERUPTED, THOUGH not immediately. The Salvadoran players had time to savor the celebration; the losers were busy letting the disappointment sink in. But it was to be a matter of days. Things ignited at dawn on July 14, in El Poy, a tiny dot on the map, a frontier town. There, the Salvadoran armed forces made the first move and crossed the border. They called it *guerra de legitima defensa* (a war of self-defense) pointing to the violence suffered by farmers who had been dispossessed and forced to flee. Diplomats lacked adequate means to halt the conflict.

The first military planes took off for Tegucigalpa. Bombs were dropped on the capital, destroying buildings and annihilating civilians and animals. Kapuściński, the one Western reporter present in the Honduran capital, wrote, "At dusk a plane flew over the city and dropped a bomb. The boom was heard everywhere. The city was gripped by panic. People took refuge in doorways, merchants shuttered their stores, cars were abandoned in the middle of the streets. At one point the lights went out and all of Tegucigalpa was plunged into darkness."

The infantry was also on the move, a signal that triggered the ground offensive. The Salvadoran army advanced, gaining miles of territory. It already looked like a decisive breach, given that El Salvador's troops outnumbered the enemy six-to-one. Honduras's response came the next day and was entrusted to the air force, where the balance of power was reversed. The attack destroyed one-fifth of the enemy fuel reserves. More raids would follow in the Salvadoran skies.

What was supposed to be a matter of form turned out to be far more complicated in practice. An unsolvable puzzle. Tegucigalpa's counteroffensive compelled the enemy forces to retreat. At 10:00 p.m. on July 18, the OAS, or Organization of American States, imposed a ceasefire. Honduras agreed; El Salvador stalled while waiting for the United States to provide them with the aircraft they needed to regain the upper hand over their enemy. The aircraft would eventually arrive, but by then it wouldn't matter.

History books place the end of the conflict on the evening of July 18, although sporadic clashes would go on until August 5, when Salvadoran forces finally retreated behind their borders. One hundred hours of conflict left six thousand dead. Over time, more shocking details emerged, from the use of napalm to mass executions.

All over a soccer match. Or was it? Rodríguez, the Pipe, the man who scored the decisive goal in the Azteca playoff, had an ambassador uncle posted in Madrid. At the end of the conflict, he stuffed an envelope with newspaper articles and sent it to his nephew. And that was how Rodríguez learned that, according to the international press, his goal had triggered the war. It was enough to keep him up all night, plagued with guilt. But were those reports true, Señor Rodríguez?

"Not a chance. The war was coming one way or another. Nothing and no one could have changed the course of history."

But in hindsight, knowing what happened next, would you still put the ball in the net?

"Of course. I'd do it all over again, from the first minute to the last. I was a striker and scoring was my job."

That was how Rodríguez responded to questions from journalist Klaus Ehringfeld. But the latter wasn't satisfied with having tracked down one of the stars of that match forty years later, in 2009. He kept digging. He tried to investigate the matter of Amelia Bolaños, as did other reporters. People spent weeks, sometimes months, in the country trying to find out more about those dramatic days, especially about the account of the eighteen-year-old girl who committed suicide after the first of three qualifying matches. After Kapuściński's report, a few even identified her as the daughter of a Salvadoran army general.

Neither Ehringfeld nor others found any trace of an

Amelia Bolaños who died the evening of June 8, 1969. No suicide was reported in the newspapers; no state funeral was attended by government representatives and the national soccer team that had just returned from Tegucigalpa. Nothing at all. Had the legendary Polish war reporter made it all up? It's impossible to know for sure, not least because Kapuściński died in 2007. There is no record of his ever having revisited the story, so what he wrote in *The Soccer War*, a book published in 1978 that details his time in Honduras, is all we have. Maybe others told him the story, and he reported it without bothering to check the facts. Or maybe he embellished it with made-up details rather than providing a factual account. Anything's possible. Ultimately it doesn't matter too much; he remains a great journalist, just as a war lasting one hundred hours and leaving six thousand dead remains absurdly tragic.

In the end, El Salvador went to the World Cup in Mexico. It played three matches and lost them all—against the host team, against Belgium, and against the Soviet Union. It allowed ten goals and scored none. Each match was played at the same stadium, the Azteca. Today, passersby can't avoid walking by the plaque commemorating the 4–3 match between Italy and Germany. *El partido del siglo* (the match of the century). Schnellinger's goal at the ninetieth minute, those riveting extra minutes ending with the delicious instep from Rivera that sent Germany's keeper one way and the ball another . . . Well, maybe there ought to be a space reserved for another plaque, one honoring another match. It wouldn't have to say much: JUNE 27, 1969. EL SALVADOR VS. HONDURAS. 3–2. Whether or not it started a war is of secondary importance. At least it would pay tribute to all those people who died for nothing.

CHAPTER 7

THE "GHOST" MATCH:
CASZELY, CHILE, AND PINOCHET'S COUP

MATCH
Chile vs. Soviet Union

FINAL SCORE
2–0 (by forfeit)

WHEN
November 21, 1973

WHERE
Estadio Nacional, Santiago

THE REFEREE BLOWS the starting whistle and Chile launches into action. The ball is driven forward by the footwork of Captain Francisco Valdés. Behind him is the team's back line, led by Elías Figueroa. Orchestrating the attack in midfield is the best man among them, Carlos Caszely. His teammates keep looking for him, hoping to give him the honor of sliding the ball in the net, but he has another idea. He'd like the captain to do the job. And Valdés does, putting Chile up by 1. A mere seventeen seconds have elapsed and Chile is already ahead.

Close your eyes for a minute and picture the description of this goal in the richly inflected telling of a Chilean radio commentator. It's a match like no other, that of November 21, 1973; what's at stake is a berth at the following year's World Cup. There's hardly enough time to take a seat in the stands before Chile is up 1–0. How is that even possible? Did a great champion cast his spell? No, that's not it. What has happened is that only one team has taken the pitch. The other team, the Soviet Union, has stayed home. In short, in Santiago that day, Chile is playing alone.

TO UNDERSTAND THE story behind the match, we need to turn back the clock.

On September 11, seventy days before the match, General Augusto Pinochet led a coup and took control of Chile. The government of the socialist Salvador Allende, elected president of the Republic three years earlier in a free and fair election, collapsed at dawn when the air force shelled the Palacio de La Moneda, headquarters of the executive branch. The army finished the job with tanks and soldiers trundling through the streets to ferret out any adversaries. Many died during the coup, including Allende. In all likelihood he took his own life so as not to end up in the hands of Pinochet's men. He may even have used the rifle Fidel Castro had given him. The end of Allende and his loyalists was the culmination of an economic crisis lasting many months that brought tens of thousands of families to their knees amid protracted strikes, galloping inflation, and a shortage of basic necessities.

While Chile was swept up in a never-ending drama, its

national team was, in the most striking of contrasts, about to fly to Moscow for a soccer match. FIFA's qualification process stipulated that one of the sixteen slots in the following year's World Cup was reserved for the winner of a playoff between teams from different continents: in this case, Chile and the Soviet Union. One newly fascist country versus the leader of the Communist bloc. You couldn't dream of a worse scenario, however much you and every other soccer guru might wish to separate the sport from politics. The first game was set for Wednesday, September 26, fifteen days after the coup. Rumors started to spread that the tiebreaker might be skipped, but if that happened FIFA would still have a slot to fill. It was too complicated. In the end, Pinochet himself withdrew the reservation, perhaps hoping to lend a veneer of normalcy to what was decidedly abnormal.

Chile embarked for Moscow aboard a military plane. It was the start of an interminable journey, with stops in Rio de Janeiro, Panama, Mexico City, and Zurich. Between stops they played two friendlies, one against Mexico's national team and the other against Switzerland's Neuchâtel Xamax FCS. At the Moscow airport, Carlos Caszely and Elías Figueroa were detained for a few hours. Why? Discrepancies in their passport photos, allegedly. The South American team should have had on their bench Rudi Gutendorf—a German globe-trotter in the true sense of the word—who would go on to have a long career coaching in over thirty countries. But Gutendorf wasn't there. He had never hidden his sympathies for Allende, and once he caught a whiff of a coup, he decided it would be best to leave Chile. He was replaced by Luis Álamos. But the team had another problem.

There have been *many* players who have, over time, embraced Salvador Allende's cause. Chief among them was the talented forward Carlos Caszely, the son of a Hungarian-born railroader. They called him "the king of the square meter" because of his ability to create opportunities for goals in tight spaces. For the past few months he had been playing in Spain, at Levante, the first leg of a career that would also take him to Barcelona where he played for Espanyol. Before emigrating, he had carried Colo-Colo to the final of the Copa Libertadores, South America's Champions Cup, which only lost in its playoff against Argentina's Independiente: a milestone never before achieved by a Chilean team.

Caszely wasn't the only one who openly sided with the former president. Alongside him was the captain, Francisco Valdés, more friend than teammate. Pinochet couldn't bear the fact that there were members on the national team with views opposed to his own, but someone must have whispered in his ear that, without them, Chile didn't stand a chance.

The first part of the World Cup playoff was celebrated in Lenin Stadium, manned as never before by law enforcement. This, despite there not being a fan among them from Chile. Diplomatic relations between the two countries had frozen in the wake of Pinochet's coup; tensions were at an all-time high. On Leonid Brezhnev's orders, the match was not to be televised; the recap was entrusted to the few print journalists who managed to get accreditation. There was even a rumor that the players would be held hostage so that they could be swapped with Chilean political prisoners. But it was just a rumor.

The thermometer registered five below zero. The Soviet Union was not a bad team. On the contrary, it had made it to the finals of the European Championship the year before and had a young striker, Oleg Blokhin, who was gaining widespread attention. If there was a favored team, it definitely wasn't Chile, yet the South Americans held the fort: defensive totem Figueroa played a game of great substance. The main casualty was Blokhin, the number one danger; the referee, Brazilian Armando Marques, turned a blind eye—or maybe two—to the blatant fouls the striker endured. After time was called, Hugo Gasc, the only Chilean journalist present, would remark, "Fortunately the referee was an avid anti-Communist. Together with Francisco Fluxá, our team leader, we had convinced him that he could not make us lose in Moscow. And he did indeed help us."

The final score was 0–0. Everything was premised on the next match. In such cases, it is customary for the two teams to meet a couple of weeks later, but in this case as many as eight weeks passed. For starters, they had to decide where the match would be played. For the Chileans, it was a no-brainer: the Estadio Nacional, the facility that had always hosted the national team's matches. It was the same stadium that hosted Brażil and Czechoslovakia for the 1962 World Cup final, when Pelé was sidelined with an injury and Garrincha put in a sublime performance.

After September 11, 1973, the day Pinochet took power, the Estadio Nacional was completely transformed. It became a principal site where opponents of the regime were imprisoned, tortured, and killed. Like an open-air concentration camp. For those who have seen the movie *Missing*, nothing more need be said. For those who haven't or don't remember it, *Missing* is filmmaker Costa-Gavras's masterpiece. An American journalist, played by Jack Lemmon, scours the stadium looking for his son, whom he fears has been arrested by the military junta. He'll never see his boy again: he was killed in a room underneath the stadium and subsequently buried inside its walls. The same fate befell untold numbers of people, especially young people, those who prior to the coup may very well have gone to the stadium to cheer on their favorite team, but in that same place met a horrible fate.

Would they hold the Chile–Soviet Union rematch at the Estadio Nacional? Any third party would have considered it madness. Between the pitch, the stands, and the underground rooms, there were thousands of prisoners who would have to be moved. Not to mention what the world would later discover thanks to foreign journalists, who eagerly waited for the planes to stop dropping bombs and the tanks to slow their tragic march so they could describe the turmoil in detail. Which is what Mario Cervi, the *Corriere della Sera* correspondent in Santiago, did. "The National Stadium," he wrote,

> is a giant modern bowl, with expensive equipment that, because of soccer mania, now even the poorest countries feel compelled to pay for. I arrive in the early afternoon to find a crowd of a few hundred people lined up outside the entrance, about thirty meters from the fences. A tense silence fills the air. Behind the gate, soldiers brandish submachine guns. In a recess that runs along the entire perimeter of the stadium, a crowd is swarming, closely guarded by other soldiers. These are the prisoners, and outside are the relatives of individuals who have been rounded up or disappeared, anxiously looking for news.

Chronicles of a normal day in Chile at the end of September. Would it really be possible to have the second match of the playoff, scheduled for November 21, at the Estadio Nacional? In those conditions? The FIFA managers were starting to wonder. They ran the risk of exposing themselves to grave embarrassment. The time had come to play the diplomacy card. The first talks between the representatives of the two federations were held at FIFA headquarters in Zurich and afterward by telegram.

It was immediately clear the dialogue was at cross-purposes. The Soviet Union asked to play on neutral ground; Chile refused. On strictly sportsmanship grounds, the South Americans had a point: "If we came all the way to Moscow, why shouldn't Moscow return the visit to Santiago?" There was also the suggestion of moving the stadium, perhaps to an outlying area like Viña del Mar or Valparaíso. The idea was floated by the heads of the Chilean federation, but the military wouldn't hear of it. It was Santiago or nothing.

In the end, FIFA broke the stalemate. They sent a small delegation composed of the Swiss secretary Helmut Käser and the Brazilian vice president Abilio d'Almeida to the capital. The pair arrived on October 23 and the following day visited the Estadio Nacional. They walked the pitch, keeping a safe distance from the stands, where some of the prisoners were stationed. The others had been locked up below the field. Käser and d'Almeida avoided contact with all those opponents of the regime who might have had stories to tell, even if telling them meant they faced certain death. The military explained to the men from FIFA that the stands where all those people were crowded was nothing more than a processing center for individuals apprehended without documents. A child could see through their story.

A few days later, FIFA issued a statement: "Based on what they saw and heard in Santiago, Mr. d'Almeida and Dr. Käser have come to the conclusion that life in the Chilean capital has returned to normal and that the guarantees given by the government authorities are such that the match between Chile and the Soviet Union can be played as scheduled on November 21. The visiting delegation has been guaranteed maximum security and from now until the day of the event the risk of things escalating is inconceivable." In the end, the vote by the German World Cup organizing committee on November 2 was fifteen in favor, three abstentions, three against.

That settled the matter for FIFA: the Chile–Soviet Union match would be played in Santiago. As for all those poor detainees, tortured and killed at the Estadio Nacional? It was, they said, fake news pushed by the pro-Communist press . . .

Meanwhile, there came a wave of protests from Moscow. Satellite states were also making themselves heard, starting with East Germany: "Since the stadium in Santiago has become a concentration camp, the match might as well be played in Dachau." Zurich didn't appear to find that funny; besides, the GDR was no bed of roses. With each passing day, room for diplomacy contracted. Russia's TASS news agency published a statement from the Soviet Football Federation that effectively closed off any possibility for maneuvering: "Following the fascist coup d'état, a climate of terror and repression has been established in Chile, and with it a campaign of provocation has been launched against the socialist countries and all democratic forces. At this time, we cannot play in a stadium stained with the blood of Chilean patriots." Switzerland took note and prepared to apply Article 22 of the World Cup regulations, which states that if a team refuses to play a match, points will be awarded to the opposing team, and the refusing team shall be expelled from the tournament.

After that, Italy's *Gazzetta dello Sport* sent their Swiss correspondent Rinaldo Giambonini to Zurich to interview Käser. Here's what he had to say: "The rules leave no room for doubt: only force majeure events are acceptable reasons for not playing. We went to Chile to get a sense of the situation. In our report, we reached the conclusion, based on real data, that the match could be played there. This meant that force majeure no longer applied."

WEDNESDAY, NOVEMBER 21, 6:00 p.m. There were just shy of twenty thousand people in the stands of the Estadio Nacional. To use a favorite term of soccer journalists, a massive *turnover* had taken place: the prisoners were swapped for ordinary people, who may have gone to the stadium harboring hopes of obtaining information on relatives or friends who had been missing since the day of the coup. Opponents of the regime had either been transferred elsewhere or taken underground, at a safe distance from prying eyes. Above the scoreboard were the words: CHILE IS UNITED TODAY BY THE YOUTH AND SPORTS. What youth? Those whom a ruthless regime had wiped off the face of the earth?

Chile donned its traditional red jersey. Had the Soviet Union also been on the field, there would have been confusion, since their colors were the same, but the Soviets were not there. There was, however, a referee on the pitch, ready to start the most absurd match in the history of the sport. It's a point worth pausing over. Who was the referee that day? I asked FIFA for clarification and their press office replied that there was no match report for that day in the Zurich archives, and therefore it was impossible to find out the name of the referee. However, many sources mention the name

Erich Linemayr, an Austrian born in 1933, and one of the most reliable referees of the time. Carlos Caszely, who we'll talk about more at length later, also mentioned him several times: "That day I would have gladly walked off the field, but referee Linemayr informed us the game still had to begin. At that point we passed the ball back and forth until our captain Francisco Valdés kicked it into an empty goal."

So, according to Caszely, Linemayr was the referee. *La Gazzetta dello Sport*, which printed a brief write-up of the so-called match, concurred. Sometime later, Linemayr would return to the subject in an interview republished by the Austrian website oepb.at, where, he explained:

> On the one hand I was happy to have been asked to referee a match that important. On the other hand I was concerned about what was going on in Chile. My wife tried to dissuade me from taking the trip, but ultimately I decided to go. I was still an international referee and I had an obligation to fulfill. It was not until I had arrived at the stadium that I was told the Soviet Union hadn't shown up. So I told the officials present that the match couldn't be played. One of them begged me to go ahead and blow the starting whistle. He was being pressured from above—meaning from the government and FIFA.

Pictures of that keeper-less goal are easy to find online. At a certain point you can also see the referee, though he is not recognizable except for the traditional (at the time) black uniform. According to the rules, the team that conceded the goal should have put the ball back into play. As the team in question wasn't there, the referee had no choice but to blow the whistle for full time. Chile won the match 2–0 by forfeit and received a pass for the World Cup the following year, while the Soviet Union was fined by FIFA for not taking the field.

LET'S SKIP AHEAD to 2007. There was less than a year to go until the final phase of the European Championship, organized by Austria and Switzerland. Austria's national team automatically qualified and therefore only played in friendlies. On September 11 (a date we've already come across in this story), Austria was scheduled to play Chile. A journalist from the APA press agency, Edgar Schütz, decided to interview Erich Linemayr. It wasn't a bad idea, seeing as the former referee represented one of the few connections in the history of soccer between the two countries. Schütz wanted to hear about that day in 1973, about that match, which was over before it started. "Sorry," Linemayr responded coolly, "I can't help you. I wasn't in Chile that day."

The journalist pressed him. What about all the stories that implicate you? Why would Caszely mention you by name?

"I don't know what to tell you. I should have refereed the

game, but once I learned that the Soviets wouldn't be showing up, I did the only thing there was to do. I returned the plane tickets and stayed home."

Erich Linemayr died in 2016, at the age of eighty-three, and took his secret, if it can be called a secret, to the grave. We're left with two opposing versions of the story. I asked Schütz about his 2007 interview. He told me he remembered a man who was convinced of what he was saying, perfectly lucid. The former referee's daughter corroborated her father's story. "I can confirm that my father did not go to Chile," she said. So what are we to make of the detailed account of November 21, 1973, of the starting whistle, the goal into an unguarded net, the match that was over before it had begun? The question is difficult, if not impossible, to answer. The man dressed in black seen in the background in the photographs of Valdés's goal might have been Linemayr or someone else; the Chilean referee Rafael Hormázabal Diaz, for instance. There are sources that say he refereed that non-match.

Why linger on this question? If Hormázabal had in fact blown the starting whistle, then the match at the Estadio Nacional was even more of a sham. When has there ever been an official match, in this case a qualifying match for the World Cup, refereed by someone from the same country as one of the two national teams on the field?

Either way, a soccer match was played that day. In a corner of the field, waiting for the farce to end, was Brazil's Santos Futebol Clube, dressed and ready to play. Apparently, the Chilean authorities had been clear about it for a while: if the Soviet Union wouldn't take the field, they'd implement Plan B by inviting a world-famous team for a high-profile friendly, so that ticket buyers wouldn't go home disappointed. They may have been called Santos, but what one heard was Pelé. Though "O Rei" wasn't there that day, the Brazilians still won 5–0.

There is another question hovering over the events of November 21, 1973. It concerns Carlos Caszely. The fiercest Chilean player of the time, perhaps ever, was also a staunch supporter of Salvador Allende, and just a few months prior to the coup he had openly campaigned for two candidates of Unidad Popular, the socialist party led by the late president of the Republic. If Caszely represented the team's "critical consciousness," why would he not take the chance to rebel against the will of the military, who were making a clean sweep of the country by eliminating anyone who opposed the regime? All it would have taken was a simple gesture: kicking the ball into the stands instead of passing it to Captain Valdés to score the easiest of goals. "The saddest goal," as many have called it. That's easy to say for a neutral observer half a century on. But what consequences would the player have faced? On the eve of the Moscow match, the regime had already stuck out its cleats. "Watch what you say" was its message to the players. Otherwise, there could be consequences for your families. They couldn't have been clearer. Perhaps when it came time to decide what to do on the pitch of the Estadio Nacional, Caszely lost his nerve.

Perhaps he and Valdés talked about it and in the end decided not to intervene. Years later, Caszely himself admitted, "If I had had the courage, I would have sent the ball elsewhere. But I had no courage that day." Can anyone really blame him and Valdés for having obeyed the will of the regime?

Augusto Pinochet remained in power for seventeen years, until 1990, perpetrating many more crimes against humanity. During those years, he crossed paths with Carlos Caszely a couple of times. The first was a few days after the drama at the Estadio Nacional. The general had insisted on meeting the national team to offer his congratulations. (For what exactly?) "At a certain point I heard footsteps," the player recounted on the website goal.com,

> and the door to the room, where we had been told to sit, opened. In walked Pinochet, with that repulsive expression on his face. He looked like the devil. I could never shake hands with that murderer. He held out his hand and waited for me to do the same. I looked him in the eye and said: "You know, don't you, how much pain you caused all those prisoners?" He covered his ears with his hands and said: "Don't talk to me about that, I don't want to know anything about it." The scene only lasted a few seconds, but it felt like hours to me. As a human being, I had an obligation. I could feel the weight of the entire Chilean people on my shoulders. I don't

> consider myself a violent person, I would never lower myself to the level of someone who kills. But in the moment, I had to say what I thought.

A few months later it was the same scene, the same players. Chile was on its way to the World Cup in Germany, and Pinochet was greeting them. He shook hands with all but one. It isn't hard to guess who.

Caszely would pay dearly for his actions. One day, on his return to Chile during a stopover in the Spanish championship, he was met at the airport by his father and sister. Something was off, and at one point Caszely asked if anything had happened. "We'll explain everything when we get home," they said. His mother was there waiting for him, and in tears she told him that she had been arrested and tortured by the regime's secret police. "I didn't want to believe it," said Caszely, "I told her not to kid around. And then she showed me the marks on her body." Pinochet had taken revenge for being snubbed.

Caszely played in two World Cups. In the first, in 1974, he is mostly remembered for being ejected in a match against West Germany after a retaliatory foul committed against Berti Vogts. It was the first time a red card had been waved at the top international competition. And because Chile's next match was against the other Germany—the East—some who sided with the dictator put two and two together and concluded that the player had gotten himself ejected on purpose to avoid having to face his Communist "brothers."

For Caszely's second World Cup—in 1982 in Spain—he is associated with a missed penalty kick against Austria. Once again, the regime's press accused him of having deliberately missed to defy Pinochet.

The beginning of the end for the dictator began with a 1988 referendum asking Chileans to vote on whether to keep the regime in power. Times had changed, and Pinochet's opponents had the right to be heard, too. In one television commercial aired during the campaign, a woman in her sixties recounted the torture she had endured and urged people to vote no. Then Carlos Caszely appeared and reiterated why people should cast a ballot against the regime: "For a tomorrow in which we can live in a free and healthy democracy. For this beautiful lady is my mother." The nos won 55 percent of the vote. And Caszely finally began to shed the weight of that goal scored at a stadium that had been transformed into a concentration camp and torture chamber.

ZAIRE

CHAPTER 8

FREE KICK IN REVERSE:
AFRICA IN THE 1970S, DECOLONIZATION, DICTATORS, AND NEOCOLONIALISM

MATCH
Brazil vs. Zaire

FINAL SCORE
3–0

WHEN
June 22, 1974

WHERE
Gelsenkirchen, Parkstadion

STAY PUT, JOSEPH. *Do what your teammates are doing. Stick to the wall. It's best for everyone.* Who knows if, in the heat of the moment, Joseph can hear those words. But Rivelino, the great Rivelino, is taking the ball and placing it on the penalty mark. If free kicks are a college subject, the mustachioed Brazilian midfielder—No. 10, a number inherited from Pelé—would no doubt be department chair; he's the best free-kick taker around. The clock is ticking, there are five minutes to go. Zaire is down 3–nil; it's time to gamble. For the Africans, a loss would be the most humiliating thing imaginable.

Maybe that's why Joseph Mwepu Ilunga won't hear of standing still. To everyone's shock he breaks free of the defensive line, dashes for the ball, and punts it as far as he can, as if the free kick were his and not his opponent's. He almost hits the astonished Rivelino square in the face. No one, not the thirty-six thousand spectators in Gelsenkirchen's Parkstadion, nor the people tuning in from every corner of the planet, can believe their eyes. The match thus far has been worthy of the 1974 Soccer World Cup, but this is a farce. And it is inevitably followed by the referee, Romanian Nicolae Rainea, waving a yellow card in the African defender's face. Just a warning. It could have been worse.

And what became of the mustachioed No. 10's free kick? It was poorly executed, as if that strange event had drained Roberto Rivelino of his superpowers.

THE BEGINNING OF the story that connects the "before" and "after" of that strange moment is enough to send a shiver down your spine. It is a story of passion, terror, and pain—both physical and emotional. To tell it, one has to go all the way back to the 1966 World Cup.

In those years Africa coveted a spot in the World Cup, and by spot we mean a place, at least one, among the world champion finalists. The tournament was being held in England, and it was still a World Cup with sixteen teams, Europe accounting for the lion's share. The few spots left were reserved for South America. People protested, but FIFA turned a deaf ear: "Dear Africans, the most we can do is allow you to compete with the representatives of Asia and Oceania for a spot among the sixteen finalists." That, in a nutshell, was the message from Zurich. The African federations were having none of it and decided to boycott the qualifiers. They pulled all their national teams, a dramatic gesture that didn't go unnoticed. The championship that concluded with a final at Wembley was suddenly a little less "worldly."

The captains of the ship finally realized that something had to be done. Therefore, beginning in 1970, there would be a place in the tournament reserved for Africa every year. At the end of the regular qualifiers, it was awarded to Morocco, which did not survive the group stage but made a good impression, drawing with Bulgaria and narrowly losing to West Germany, 2–1. They had even taken the lead for a time. They were coached by Yugoslav Blagoje Vidinić, a former goalkeeper who won the Olympic title in 1960 in Rome.

After his time in Morocco, Vidinić packed his bags and moved south to sub-Saharan Africa. In 1972, he took another big gamble on Zaire's touchline. A few months prior you couldn't have located the name Zaire on a FIFA map. It was the brainchild of the dictator Joseph-Désiré Mobutu. Or, to use his full name, Mobutu Sese Seko Kuku Ngbendu Wa Za Banga, which translates to "Mobutu the almighty warrior who, because of his endurance and inflexible will to win, will go from conquest to conquest leaving fire in his wake." Mobutu had been many things in his life. For one, he'd been secretary of state and chief of staff of the army of the Republic of Congo, which was created in 1960 after the country won its independence from Belgium, culminating in half a century of looting, abuse of power, and mass murder. When democratic elections could finally be held in the country, Patrice Lumumba emerged victorious. The country that followed became the Democratic Republic of Congo. But Mobutu didn't care to play the role of faithful servant, so the ambitious soldier set to work with the CIA and the Belgian armed forces to depose the unfortunate prime minister, whose one crime was to have sought political support from Khrushchev's Soviet Union. Lumumba was, in quick succession, arrested, shot, dismembered, and dissolved in acid.

In a nation perpetually torn by political and ethnic strife, Mobutu had no trouble climbing the ladder. That culminated in 1965 in a coup d'état, which launched a reign of terror that lasted for more than thirty years. His dictatorship was bathed in the blood of many innocent people and led to the country's gradual "Africanization," including bizarre measures such as a ban on neckties and miniskirts, which were too "Western" for the tyrant's taste. Gone was the Democratic Republic of Congo; something more in keeping with African identity was called for. Hence Zaire—the original name of the Congo River.

The image Zaire presented to the world in those years was the same as many other African countries: a small group controlled much of the wealth and enjoyed unbridled luxury while most people struggled to get by. But unlike its neighbors, Zaire had immense copper and diamond mines, which made it a valuable partner for Western powers, beginning with the United States. That business would bring Mobutu a flood of money, which systematically filled the dictator's personal coffers rather than alleviating the suffering of the population.

AMONG HIS MANY characteristics, one is unquestionably relevant to the story: Mobutu Sese Seko, etc., was a huge soccer fan. He'd even played the sport in his youth. He'd been a goalkeeper and, according to those who saw him play, didn't possess much talent. To slake his thirst for power, he got it into his head to grow the sport in his country. How? Simple, by drawing on state funds to bring back all the nation's strongest players who had left to seek their fortunes in Belgium. Two teams in particular benefited from this move, Vita Club and Tout Puissant Englebert (later Mazembe). Many years on, in 2010, the latter team would reach the Club World Cup finals and lose to Inter Milan, the latter fresh off its famous triplet.

But let's turn back the clock to the end of the 1960s. The Democratic Republic of Congo, which had not yet changed its name, was beginning to rack up wins on the continent, first with its clubs and then with its national team. Tout Puissant—not yet Mazembe—was awarded the African Champions Cup two years in a row, in 1967 and 1968. The latter was also the year of the country's first victory in the Africa Cup of Nations, the tournament for national teams, hosted that year by Ethiopia. It was a time of transformation; in 1971, the country changed its name to Zaire—but did not cease to triumph on the soccer pitch. This was in no small part thanks to Vita Club, winner of the African Champions Cup in 1973, but was largely due to the success of the national team.

Those were heady months: first came their historic qualification for the World Cup, followed by the 1974 African Cup of Nations, played that March in Egypt. As Matteo Bruschetta recounts in his book *I Mondiali dei vinti, storie e miti delle peggiori nazionali di calcio* (Losers' World Cups: Stories and Myths of the Worst National Soccer Teams), the stars of the continental triumph flew home on the presidential plane and paraded the cup at the 20th of May Stadium in Kinshasa before thousands of delirious fans. The new African champions wore the leopard skin headdresses so beloved by Mobutu. In fact, because of the dictator's passion for the spotted feline, the players' historic name was changed from the Lions to the Leopards.

Zaire's star player was center forward Pierre Ndaye Mulamba, a genuine nightmare for African defenses. His uncanny gift for scoring goals earned him the nickname Mutumbula, the Assassin—a clear allusion to his killer moves in the penalty area. In Congolese folklore, Mutumbula is a white cannibal who stalks and eats black children. In the six matches of the 1974 Africa Cup of Nations, Mulamba scored nine goals, a record that still stands half a century later. No one, not Samuel Eto'o or Didier Drogba or Sadio Mané or Victor Osimhen, has managed to beat it.

Mobutu was licking his lips. The national team's exploits

were manna for a country being scrutinized by the international community—even more so for its dictator. There had to be a parade in the presidential palace, of course, for the host to show off his largesse. He gave each player an apartment, a Volkswagen Passat, and the promise of a check for forty-five thousand dollars, a figure that made the heads of young people, used to living with much less, spin. *Excuse me, Mr. President, but when will we see that money? Soon, soon. In the meantime, focus on getting in the best shape possible for the World Cup in Germany.* Who knows if Mobutu's words were a comfort to the players. At that moment they likely were, if what Mwepu—he of the penalty kick folly—said years later was true: "For us Mobutu was like a father. When he received us and announced the prizes for winning the African Cup of Nations, his generals were so envious that he had to give them a car too."

ON THE DAY it won the African Cup, Zaire already knew who it would face in the World Cup. The draw was not particularly favorable: two European teams, Scotland and Yugoslavia, and, worse still, the world champions, Brazil. True, Pelé was no longer there, but the names Jairzinho and Rivelino would keep anybody up at night. In short, things didn't look good for Zaire. Yet for some reason, in the corridors of power in Kinshasa, someone had gotten it into their head that qualifying for the second round, and with it entry into the "G8" of football, was achievable. That was, to put it mildly, wishful thinking.

Mind you, the national team was heroic, even if "only" on the African continent, displaying an interesting combination of physicality and technique. Filippo Maria Ricci, who knows African football like the back of his hand, listed the players and their nicknames in the magazine *Linea Bianca*: "Lobilo, aka The Doctor; Kembo, Mr. Goal; God of the Ball Kakoko; Little Wizard Mavuba; Ntumba the Flea; Mayanga, whose nickname, Goodyear, alluded to how many yards he could cover on the field without losing air; and Caravel Mbungu, who like that Portuguese ship, always strove to 'land.'" And then there was Mulamba the Murderer, of course, but also the Volvo because he was as reliable as the Swedish car.

"Operation Germany" began in Switzerland. The team pitched its tent beside Lake Lucerne for the first phase of the World Cup training camp. But the temperature never rose above forty degrees Fahrenheit—a far cry from the hundred-degree weather in and around Kinshasa. Therefore, the federation decided to travel three hundred miles south, to Coverciano, in southeastern Florence. Three friendlies were quickly arranged. Zaire lost two of them, to Fiorentina and Roma, and tied in the third, against Cesena. It was not auspicious. There were still strategical kinks to work out and less and less time before the start of the World Cup.

In their favor was a combination of enthusiasm and curiosity that always attends new arrivals in soccer. Zaire had nothing to lose. Who knew, it might just stun the world. In the meantime, the team had won the hearts of Ascheberg, a municipality of ten thousand inhabitants selected to be a base camp because of its proximity to Dortmund and Gelsenkirchen, where the team would play its matches.

Walburga Krebber, who, alongside her husband Manfred, had been appointed by the organizing committee to look after the team, remembers those days very well: "They stayed in a luxury hotel, which meant that they didn't lack for funding. There was only one electronics shop in the area and the players emptied it—literally. They had a weakness for cameras. They photographed everything, and I would travel several kilometers almost every day to have the film developed and bring the photos to their hotel." Krebber was a gifted cook, and one evening she turned up at the camp with a freshly baked cherry pie. The players liked it so much that eating Frau Walburga's dessert became a daily ritual.

Ah, right, then there were the matches. The "real" World Cup matches, the first ever for a team from sub-Saharan Africa. Their debut fell on June 14, in Dortmund, against Scotland and its Ballon d'Or recipient Denis Law; the pillars of the miracle team at Leeds, Peter Lorimer and Billy Bremner; the future three-time European champion Kenny Dalglish; Joe "The Shark" Jordan—distinguished names all. But Zaire didn't cut a poor figure, and even came close to taking the lead when Etepe Kakoko, the "ball god," squared off with the goalkeeper, but came up short. It ended as expected.

"Against Scotland," Roberto Milazzo wrote in the columns of the *Corriere della Sera*, "a castle was all it took to achieve checkmate. The first Central African country to take part in the World Cup demonstrated that it has quickly picked up individual technique: it plays well with its feet (even if it shoots poorly) but not with its head. The leap of a lanky Jordan was sufficient to shatter the illusions that their confident start had roused in the stands." One goal and one assist: not a bad showing for The Shark, who would go on to play for Milan and Verona. For the record, Lorimer delivered the other goal.

I asked Jordan to search his memory of that day, and he didn't hold back:

> It was an important game for us, almost historic I'd say. Scotland hadn't been in the World Cup for sixteen years. England hadn't qualified, so we were the only ones representing Great Britain. There were lots of fans in the stands. In a half hour or so we had already clinched the win. Maybe we felt satisfied, but the fact is we started to play a sterile game of possession. That was a mistake. We should have insisted on scoring again to shore up our lead. Zaire seemed like a somewhat naïve team. For one thing, their defense completely forgot about me when I scored. And the goalkeeper let a pretty easy shot slip through his hands. But come to think of it

> we were naïve too for not attacking once we were up two. I remember toward the end I wanted to swap shirts but it was no use. None of them accepted. I got the feeling that they didn't have many disposable shirts. And that was just the first game.

Losing 2–nil to a European team in your first World Cup is no big deal. Unless your name is Mobutu and you suffer from delusions of grandeur. The dictator had already planned a concert of Woodstock proportions in Kinshasa for that fall, with icons like James Brown and B.B. King. It was meant as a prelude to the legendary Rumble in the Jungle, the world heavyweight boxing match between Muhammad Ali and George Foreman that would go down in history. Mobutu wouldn't have minded showing off a national soccer team that was among the best in the world, but a first match defeat felt like elimination to him. "If that's the way it's going to be, they can forget about the forty-five thousand dollars," the dictator thundered from his residence. And there were no assurances that those boys wouldn't face additional consequences, too.

The bad news soon reached Zaire's German training camp and immediately the team's hawks jumped at the opportunity: "We're not playing Yugoslavia." The doves responded: "This isn't a joke. If we refuse to take the field, he'll kill us and our families." They'd eventually play, of course. But how? Reluctantly, like people who have other things on their mind. They also began to suspect that the money they'd been promised had been pocketed by someone with a European bank account.

JUNE 18 WAS a day that will go down in history, at least the history of the World Cup. Just over fifteen minutes into the match, Yugoslavia was ahead 3–0. At that point, Vidinić sidelined the goalkeeper Robert Kazadi, who wasn't entirely to blame for the score, and put in Dimbi Tubilandu. The order came from above, perhaps from a government representative sitting in VIP. Poor Tubilandu, who didn't play at the level of the starting player and stood a mere five feet, five inches. He collected the first kick at the back of the net. The score was now 4–0. The Africans believed the goal should have been disallowed because the scorer, Josip Katalinski, had committed a foul. Our friend Mwepu lost his head and kicked the referee, the Colombian Delgado. Delgado didn't see the aggressor and in response expelled Mulamba, who clearly had nothing to do with it, but would wind up being disqualified for a year. They only ended the match down 9–0 because at a certain point Yugoslavia decided not to add insult to injury.

While Zaire was licking its wounds, a plane from Mobutu's fleet took off from Kinshasa airport carrying presidential guards. These men were the dictator's most loyal servants, people accustomed to embarking on the thorniest of missions. Their present brief was far less complicated. Once they arrived at the team's hotel, the agents simply had to lock the players and the technical staff in a room and relay the president's diktat: "You can lose the third match if you have to, but by three goals at most. Otherwise it'll be trouble for you and your loved ones." The third match was against Brazil, the reigning world champions, who, because they had yet to score—they'd twice drawn 0–0, against Yugoslavia and Scotland—were at risk of elimination, and therefore wouldn't be pulling any punches.

The match was scheduled for June 22 at the Parkstadion in Gelsenkirchen. Winning by three goals would suit Brazil, too. If there were a three-way tie, the goal difference would decide who advanced to the next stage. Zaire would need to tip the scales. Yugoslavia's 9–0 victory ensured their safety, whereas Scotland had "only" beaten the Leopards 2–0. This meant that if Yugoslavia and Scotland played to a draw, Brazil's Seleção would only need a three-goal victory to advance, even if they finished second in the group. Unsurprisingly, the Slavs and the Scotsmen wound up drawing 1–1.

At that point Brazil's mission was simple: to score at least three goals and concede none. With a few minutes to go, the world champions were up 3–0 thanks to goals by Jairzinho, Rivelino, and Valdomiro. Brazil was relaxed; Zaire far from it. The Kinshasa squad knew full well that if they conceded a fourth goal their lives were over.

And now we come to where we began the chapter: to the punting of the ball before Rivelino had a chance to take his kick. Many in that moment wrote it off as "typically African." And poor Mwepu Ilunga had to live with such nonsense for a good quarter of a century. We're talking about a soccer great on Africa's twentieth-century dream team. Then, one day in 2002, he set the record straight on BBC: He'd known the rules. He did what he did out of fear, pure and simple. Fear of dying, which would have been possible had Rivelino scored. He decided to kick the ball as far as he could in the hope of gaining precious seconds. Can you blame him?

IN THE END, the Kinshasa Leopards succeeded in saving their skins—but the good news stops there. In their homeland they became personae non gratae, even traitors. When they walked down the street people hardly bothered to acknowledge them. Other countries saw things differently. Mulamba, for one, was offered a chance to play for Paris Saint-Germain, but the dictator interfered and the transfer fell through.

Yes, Mulamba. His denouement is one for the books. Having lost his shot to play in Europe, the center forward pressed on and ended his career in his homeland. In 1994, twenty years after the German World Cup and more importantly after an Africa Cup of Nations, where he scored nine goals in six games, the continent's governing body invited him to Tunis to receive a commemorative medal. The buzz was fleeting. No sooner had he returned to Kinshasa than a commando of soldiers raided his house and seized the medal and all his money. Not content with their loot, they shot Mulamba and threw him off a bridge, believing him dead. His son Tridon met a worse fate. In the commotion he was struck in the head—whether by a bullet or the butt of a rifle isn't clear—and died.

Mulamba was saved by a miracle, thanks to a group of children who were playing near the bridge. Seeing him on the ground, they ran to tell their parents. Recovery is hard, there are wounds from which one doesn't heal. He couldn't stay in Zaire. In 1996, he moved to South Africa where he found lodging in a shantytown, married a local woman, and earned a living as an illegal parking attendant. In 1998, during the Africa Cup of Nations in Burkina Faso, the news arrived that he had died in a diamond mine in Angola. A minute of silence was observed during the semifinal between South Africa and the Democratic Republic of the Congo—Mulamba's present and his past. But it was a case of mistaken identity. Fake news, as we say now. Pierre Ndaye Mulamba never went to Angola. Cape Town remained his second home.

Mulamba's choice can be explained by the end of apartheid and the rise to the presidency of Nelson Mandela. His story became the subject of a book and a television documentary, publicity that brought him belated but well-deserved attention. The dictator Mobutu died in 1997—and with him the name Zaire—and the Congolese authorities offered Mulamba the opportunity to return home, promising him decent housing, but he preferred to stay where he was. After all, South Africa had given him a second lease on life. He had found a partner and had even started coaching kids from the townships, the poorest areas of Cape Town.

Pierre Mutumbula Ndaye Mulamba died in 2019, and this time it was not fake news.

ANOTHER OF HIS national teammates, "Ricky" Mafuila Mavuba, passed away prematurely in 1996. His story, too, was peculiar. Mavuba was called Little Wizard for his skill at penalty and corner kicks, yet at the 1974 World Cup he shuttled between the bench and the stands and didn't see a minute of play. Could there really not have been a spot for him, even as a substitute?

After his career ended, he started a family with an Angolan woman and moved to his wife's country, where he stayed until the outbreak of civil war forced him to flee precipitously. His destination? Europe. Any place would do. At this point, his life assumed the contours of a novel. He, his wife Therese, and their ten children, boarded a rusty scow. What's more, his wife was pregnant; the baby was due to arrive in a matter of days. And as it turned out, the baby was born, on March 8, 1984, somewhere at sea between the African coast and the Strait of Gibraltar. It was a narrowly avoided tragedy, the kind you find in newspapers today. They named the new arrival Antonio, and his father gave him a middle name, Rio, so that everyone would know he was born surrounded by water.

In France, the Mavuba family settled into a new life. Little Rio liked kicking the ball around. He joined the Bordeaux youth team and at nineteen made his Ligue 1 debut. By then his father was dead, as was his mother, and

Rio wanted nothing more than to ensure a decent future for his brothers. Thanks to soccer, he succeeded. In 2004, he debuted with the French national team despite attempts by the Congo's coach Claude Le Roy to convince him to come play for his father's home team. "France is the nation that welcomed me and my family," he said. "I could never choose another team." By the end of his career, he'd played thirteen matches in all. And the last brings the story full circle, in a way. Mavuba played the final twenty-five minutes in a match against Honduras, a qualifier for the 2014 World Cup in Brazil. That day, his father Ricky, no longer alive, was nonetheless by his side.

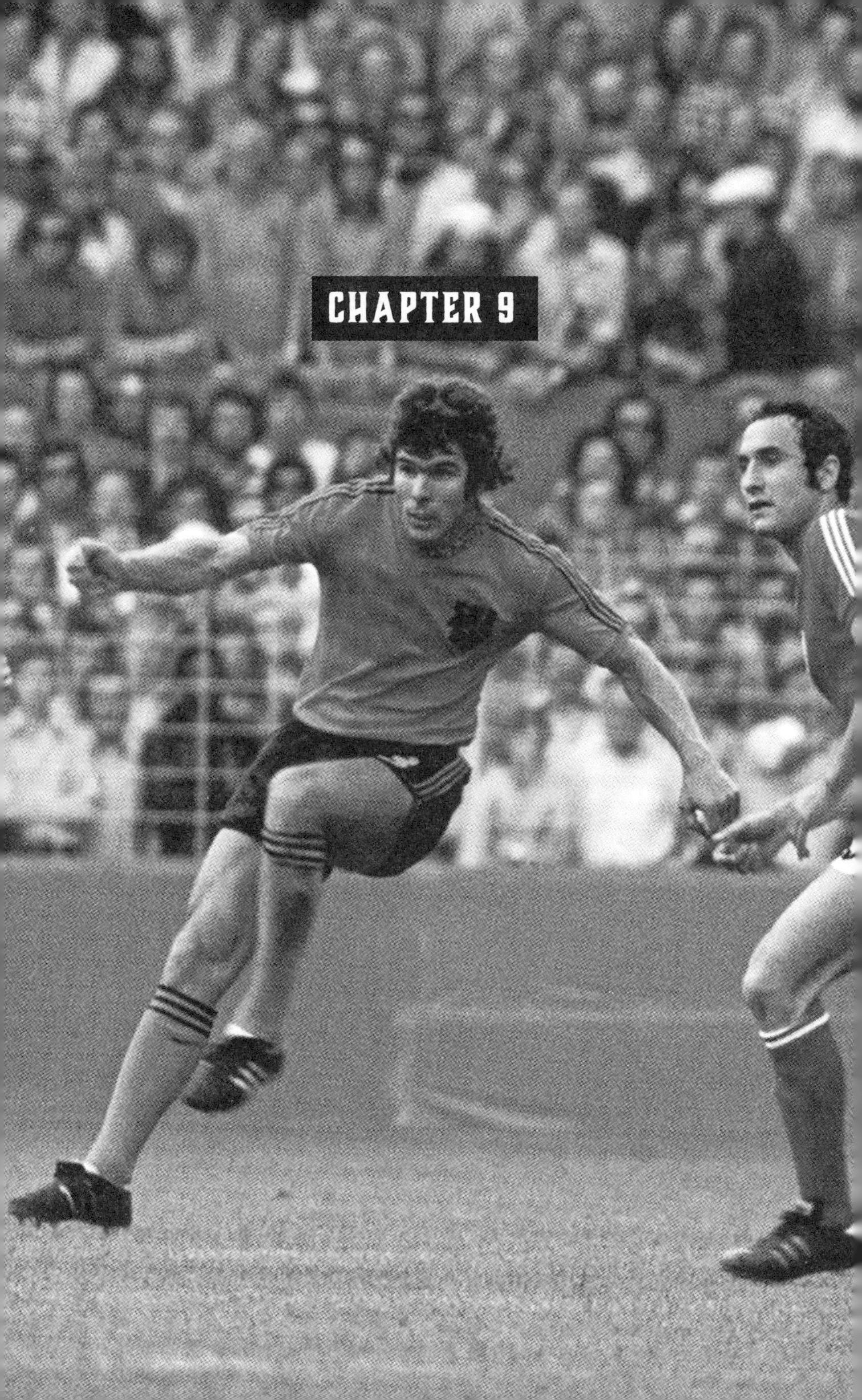

CHAPTER 9

NO PAYBACK:
GERMANY, HOLLAND, AND THE SPECTER OF NAZISM

MATCH
West Germany vs. Holland

FINAL SCORE
2–1

WHEN
July 7, 1974

WHERE
Olympiastadion, Munich

WHY THE LONG face, Wim? Give us a smile. Mother Nature gave you a gift for playing soccer. You have the best job in the world. And the pay's pretty good, too.

It's no use.

Wim lets the words slide off him and marches down the pitch. Who knows how many times he's been told that. After training. After victories and defeats. Whenever a fan asks him for his autograph. His full name is Willem van Hanegem. He symbolizes the other half of Holland, which won the hearts of millions of soccer fans in the early seventies. "Beggars for beauty," the writer Eduardo Galeano might have called them.

And beauty abounds in the country of windmills. Well, more in Amsterdam than in Rotterdam. There's Cruyff's Ajax and van Hanegem's Feyenoord. The Lancers are the better known, better loved team, but it was Feyenoord that took the first Dutch Champions Cup. In 1970, they defeated Celtic in Milan. Ajax's rise occurred later. The teams shared the same soccer DNA but came out of profoundly different cities and philosophies: Rotterdam was a city of industry; Amsterdam was one of museums, theaters, and the pursuit of a good time. The poet and writer Jules Deelder described the difference in no uncertain terms: "In Holland, money is made in Rotterdam and squandered in Amsterdam."

WIM VAN HANEGEM was born on February 20, 1944, in Breskens, a fishing village in southwestern Netherlands. He was born during the most dramatic phase of the Second World War, when the death toll kept ticking up and up. After trying to gain access to the sea and put London and Great Britain in its crosshairs, the Nazis now had to deal with the Allied forces. They'd gone from being hunters to being hunted by the British air force. The RAF bombings were relentless. On the night of September 11, 1944, sirens filled the skies, prompting civilians to seek refuge in air-raid shelters. But for some members of the van Hanegem family it was too late. Wim wasn't seven months old; he was too young to realize what was happening. His mother somehow managed to get him to safety, but there was nothing she could do for his father and sister and one of his brothers. They were buried under the bombs. English bombs, true. But had the Nazis not invaded four years earlier, it never would have happened.

And to think that between the Dutch and the Germans things had gone smoothly for centuries. They'd been excellent neighbors, with little tension between them. In the world of soccer, after the First World War, it didn't take long for the two federations to re-establish relations. Their national teams had squared off again in 1923, well in advance of other matches, for example Germany vs. England. Even after the rise of Nazism in the 1930s, the Dutch were convinced they had nothing to fear, that their German neighbors would never attack them. In no time, things had changed completely.

Nobody expected the 1940 invasion. It was a bolt from the blue. First off, once they crossed the border, the Wehrmacht soldiers seized people's bicycles. The full-scale confiscation deprived tens of thousands of people of their only means of transportation. Then came the arrests of the Jews. In five years, roughly one hundred thousand people were deported to concentration camps. From deportations to bombings to what history would ultimately refer to as the *Hongerwinter* (the winter of hunger) which exacted a heavy toll: twenty thousand people died, mostly from starvation. Everything was scarce, even bread. The few people who didn't have bicycles taken would trek dozens of miles and then return home with whatever they had managed to get their hands on, sometimes no more than a sack of potatoes. The bare minimum needed to survive.

Wim van Hanegem would learn all this years later from the stories of those who had survived the bombings and the winter of hunger. He must have come to the simple conclusion that Germany was to blame for everything, including the death of his father, brother, and sister. It didn't matter that the British had been the ones to drop the bombs. For him, Germans and Nazis were synonymous. Not even his passion for soccer was able to lessen his pain and resentment.

ON THE PITCH, van Hanegem was a diesel engine: slow to crank—not a paragon of elegance. His ungainly way of moving on the field earned him the nickname De Kromme, "the Crooked One." To make up for it, whenever he kicked the ball, he seemed to have radar in his feet. Or rather, in his left foot. He knocked on the doors of several clubs, but none gave him the time of day. At sixteen he settled for playing on Velox, a minor team out of Utrecht. During training, he stood behind one of the goals to watch, and every now and then the ball arrived in his direction. He would send it back into play with a style all his own, systematically kicking it with the outside of his foot. The unpredictable trajectories he created impressed the coaches and ultimately secured him a place on the team. His ascendancy took time. He wouldn't join Feyenoord until 1968, when he was twenty-four years old, but he would be there to play a leading role during the most riveting chapters in the history of the Rotterdam club. His coach and mentor, Ernst Happel, would say of him: "He plays every game as if it were his last, as if it were a matter of life and death." Life, death: it always comes back to that.

The next step in van Hanegem's soccer career was the national team. If soccer were a government, the Netherlands at that time would be a single party—Ajax—with Feyenoord playing a minor role, thanks to van Hanegem; his best friend, the midfielder Wim Jansen; and a little later the center back Wim Rijsbergen. But the caliphs of Amsterdam run the show. One in particular: No. 14.

Johan Cruyff commanded as if from a cloud and delivered instructions to his teammates: "You go fifteen feet wide." "You go thirty forward to signal for the pass." The man was like a manager. More than a manager. This was the birth of *totaalvoetbal* (total football) a revolutionary strategy in a soccer culture that is, at the end of the day, conservative. The fullbacks attacked. The wingers lent a hand from behind. No one stuck to their original position. The pace was frenetic, the pressing ferocious, the regaining of the ball immediate. This is how Ajax won the European Cup three times in a row, from 1971 to 1973.

Now it was the national team's turn. The Netherlands had only participated in the World Cup once, in 1938, when they lost 3–0 to Czechoslovakia and were immediately sent home. This time it was a totally different situation. Ajax and Feyenoord were the top teams in the European Club, having replaced Real Madrid, Inter Milan, and Manchester United.

And players from those teams made up the majority of the national team.

Nor was it insignificant that the 1974 World Cup was played in West Germany. Wim van Hanegem was not the type to give free rein to his mood or his emotions. He kept it all inside, smiled little if at all, and preferred silence to words. Every now and then he would think back to his mother's stories, to the bombing that took the lives of his family: "All the suffering those damned Germans caused. Thirty years gone, and now it's my turn to make them feel it."

It was an understandable aim, though the Dutch almost wound up watching the World Cup on TV. The final qualifier, on November 18, 1973, saw Holland facing off against Belgium. Both teams entered the match tied on points in the standings, with the Netherlands poised to qualify on superior goal difference if the game ended in a draw. In the eighty-ninth minute, Belgium earned a free kick. Paul van Himst—the man often hailed as Brussels's answer to Cruyff—took it. Jan Verheyen found the ball and fired past Holland's goalkeeper Piet Schrijvers. It looked like the Netherlands would be eliminated. The referee, a Soviet named Kazakov, began to gesture to midfield. But then he stopped. Out of the corner of his eye he noticed the linesman's flag—offside. He's the only official to spot the infringement. They're back to 0–0, securing Holland's qualification. Had a VAR monitor been available at the time, it would have been Belgium going to the World Cup.

FRANTIŠEK FADRHONC IS probably not a name many people recognize. A coach, he was born in 1914 in the former Czechoslovakia, left the country with the advent of Communism, and moved to Holland, where he twice stewarded Willem II, a small provincial team, to the championship. And in 1970, somewhat surprisingly, the Football Federation entrusted him with the national team. It wasn't the obvious choice, since Holland had failed to qualify for the 1972 European Championship and came so close to missing the World Cup in Germany.

In short, with Fadrhonc at the helm, they couldn't attempt to take the World Cup. So who would suit? There was one experienced coach who would gladly accept, who knew Ajax forward and backward. You mean Rinus Michels? He's coaching Barcelona! Not a chance. Despite their reservations, the federation reached out to Michels. And he ultimately said yes. Incidentally, Johan Cruyff had also been at Barça, for a year. The two men had been the architects of Ajax's first European Cup, in 1971, then Michels had pocketed Barcelona's pesetas before his replacement by the Romanian Ștefan Kovács.

So, Michels was the man. The same coach who, years before, had slammed Wim van Hanegem. The gist of his judgment? He was too slow for the kind of game that Ajax played. Fortunately for van Hanegem, it was a minor offense. In the court of appeals, the lone presiding judge, Rinus Michels, acquitted De Kromme, declared him fit to play, and put him on the national team. Besides, giving up his physicality and pinpoint passes would have been the most damaging of self-inflicted wounds.

The Dutch had another knot to untie as they got ready for the World Cup: who to put in goal? Under normal circumstances they'd start PSV Eindhoven's Jan van Beveren, but he was hobbled by injuries, and Cruyff wasn't a fan (grounds enough for rejection). The second choice was Piet Schrijvers from Twente, but No. 14 wasn't crazy about him either. He'd go to the World Cup, but as a substitute. A substitute for whom? A man who wasn't even a professional soccer player. His name was Jan Jongbloed, a player for FC Amsterdam, the city's other club. He owned a tobacco shop; soccer, along with fishing, was merely one of his hobbies. He played once for the national team, in 1962—five minutes in a friendly against Denmark, conceded one goal, and that was that. No one could have imagined that twelve years later he would be in the starting lineup at the World Cup. Jongbloed was chosen mainly because, in the eyes of Michels and Cruyff, he possessed one important quality: his precision gave them greater flexibility in their lineup. Anyone with eyes could see he wasn't great between the goalposts, but clearly that wasn't of primary importance for the inventors of total football.

That World Cup became the stage where Dutch football would be consecrated. The team played the game they knew by heart: *totaalvoetbal*. It was like watching Ajax at its best. A national team like no other—exceptional. Between matches, Michels would sometimes fly to Barcelona to settle issues related to his contract with the Catalan club and plan for the upcoming season. The Netherlands finished the group stage with two wins and a draw, scoring six goals and conceding one. The home team, West Germany, lost the derby against their GDR neighbors and passed on to the next stage in second place. This meant that the Dutch and Western Germans could only face off in the final. Depending on how Brazil and Poland played, the prospect wasn't so far-fetched. At one of several press conferences he gave, Cruyff was asked which of the Germans could play on his team, and he didn't hold back: "[Franz] Beckenbauer maybe, goalie [Sepp] Maier, [Paul] Breitner. If I'm being generous, [Uli] Hoeness." Sorry, Cruyff, but what about Gerd Müller? "Not him. If he wanted to play for the Netherlands he'd have to learn to get back into midfield and mix it up."

In the end, the Germans and the Dutch would, indeed, face off for the title. Cruyff and his teammates secured their spot by beating Brazil 2–0 in one of the most exciting matches of the tournament. For many it was a sign of things to come. The reigning champions had been defeated by the future champions. Germany, on the other hand, had a tougher time against Poland. They met in Frankfurt, on a field that was hardly suitable for play. It was especially hard for Poland's Grzegorz Lato and Robert Gadocha, two unstoppable Polish wingers who kept getting bogged down in the mud. The winning goal was scored by none other than Gerd Müller, he whom Cruyff said didn't have the stuff to play for the Dutch. But when it came to scoring, he was second to none.

At the start of the World Cup, Rinus Michels asked his

assistant and old friend Cor van der Hart to observe the Netherlands's upcoming opponents in person. He was to go, take notes, and write up his report once he got back to training camp. But van der Hart never showed up in Frankfurt. Nor did any other member of the Dutch staff. At first no one noticed; after all, they were little known and unrecognizable. The truth wouldn't emerge until later: van der Hart had a weakness for alcohol. One day, after a glass too many, he threw a bottle of champagne out of his hotel window, missing a player's head by inches. The stunt could have ended in tragedy and wound up costing the technician his job and a ticket home. Once van der Hart was gone, nobody bothered to send an envoy to watch West Germany play Poland. Maybe it wasn't a priority, but a last look at their final opponent might have been useful . . .

Perhaps Michels didn't send anyone to Frankfurt because he had other things on his mind. On the day of Holland vs. Brazil and Germany vs. Poland, the German paper *Bild* printed a full-page headline: "Cruyff, Champagne, Naked Girls and a Cool Dip." The story detailed a pool party at the Dutch hotel that was attended by players and a group of attractive young women who, according to the report, were neither the wives nor the girlfriends of Cruyff and his teammates. Clearly, it wasn't the best way to prepare for a date with history, at least not soccer history. Michels, who from the start of the tournament never missed an opportunity to show off his excellent German, immediately refused to answer questions in the language of Goethe. "From now on," he thundered to the press pool, "and until the final, we are at war. And war comes with its own set of rules." War, war, always war.

DAVID WINNER EXPLAINS it best in his book *Brilliant Orange*: the Dutch hit upon an innovative, creative, and abstract approach to space because that is exactly what they have had to do for centuries in every aspect of life. Because of its unique geographical circumstances, Holland is a nation of "spatial neurotics." It is one of the most crowded and rigidly organized parcels of land on earth. Space in Holland is a priceless asset; every inch has been exploited and contested for centuries. Controlling the land has always been a question of national survival. A good example of this is the country's water system, which is regulated with Swiss precision because more than half of the country sits below sea level.

What does all this have to do with soccer? A lot. As has already been pointed out, total football is about optimizing space and dominating every corner of the field: the defender playing as a striker and vice versa; ruthless pressing on one's adversary when they have possession of the ball. As the English manager Dave Sexton remarked, "With their pressing and rotation, the Dutch created space where there wasn't any before." Ajax learned that lesson by heart, to what effect we know, and it earned them a place among the two or three strongest teams of all time.

There was only one piece of the puzzle missing for them, and it fell into place on the afternoon of Sunday, July 7, 1974, the day of the World Cup final. The Dutch didn't need a boost of self-confidence; that much was clear. They were sure they were the better team, and that was enough. The fact that they were playing in Munich, in the enemy's lair, didn't shake their confidence. There were six Ajax players and the same number from Bayern in the German ranks. A year earlier, the two teams had squared off in the European Cup. It had been a cakewalk for Cruyff and company, who won easily on their home turf (4–0) before losing narrowly (2–1) at the Olympiastadion in Munich. The score of the first match took the sting out of the defeat.

The Dutch were confident, the Germans afraid. The account of Bernd Hölzenbein, striker for Germany's national team, Mannschaft, was typical: "We had decided we would look them straight in the eyes in the locker-room tunnel—to show them we were on their level. They felt invincible, you could see it in their faces. While we were waiting to head out to the pitch, I tried to look them in the eye. But I failed. They made us feel inferior."

As for van Hanegem—he was van Hanegem: in a cone of silence, his gaze impenetrable, thinking back on those distant days of 1944. The opportunity he'd been waiting for all his life had finally come. Winning wasn't enough for De Kromme; he wanted to humiliate his adversary, to compensate, in however small a way, for the pain he had been carrying around for thirty years. What he didn't know, or chose to ignore, was that while Holland may have been attacked by Nazi Germany, for a long time it had winked at its invader. So much so that the Dutch National Socialist Party had the largest following outside of Germany. The Dutch economy itself did not fail to offer its support to the German war effort. One of the most illustrious collaborators was the president of the national football federation, Karel Lotsy, who had excluded Jewish players and managers from Dutch soccer well before the Nazis did.

IN MUNICH, SOMETHING unprecedented happened, at least for a World Cup final. The Dutch won the kickoff and began passing the ball around. They passed it five, ten, fifteen times. Then Cruyff decided to break the deadlock by tearing up the turf and drawing a foul from Uli Hoeness. It was a penalty kick. The other Johan—Neeskens—stepped up to the spot and didn't miss. The Netherlands took the lead. The first German to touch the ball was goalkeeper Sepp Maier, after two minutes of play: he picked it up from the back of the net and passed it to his teammates to resume play. At this point, the Dutch team formed two factions. The first, largely comprised of Ajax players, was just looking to win. It had no historical scores to settle and regarded Germany as an opponent like any other. Besides, Cruyff and Beckenbauer, the two stars on the field, were on good terms. Calling it a friendship might be an overstatement, but there was certainly mutual respect. The other faction was led by Wim van Hanegem and had a completely different mindset. For them, winning the World Cup wasn't good enough. The Germans had to be humiliated, as they had done to the Dutch thirty years earlier. How should they be humiliated? Not by scoring more goals, which was what Cruyff would have wanted. The Dutch had to mock them, hide the ball from them, make them run around in circles. Paradoxically, van Hanegem would be happy if they had won 1–0, as long as the world witnessed them embarrass Mannschaft and, by extension, its people.

While the Dutch unraveled, Germany pulled together. Nothing out of this world, but the match grew more even. Jongbloed had his work cut out for him. In the twenty-fifth minute, referee Jack Taylor called the second penalty of the day, this time in the Germans' favor. Paul "The Maoist" Breitner—who was never shy about his affection for the Chinese leader—stepped up to bury the kick. It's a tied game, back to square one. Before halftime, Gerd Müller also had his say. The goal was pure Müller: a seemingly innocuous ball from the right, but he beat his primary defender Rijsbergen to it, spun sharply, and sent it into the far corner of the goal. It wasn't pretty—Müller never scored pretty goals—but it mattered tremendously. Van Hanegem was beside himself. Some people swore that at the end of the first half they saw him pick up the ball and hurl it at the referee. All that's certain is that Taylor pulled out a yellow card, but he pointed it at Cruyff, not De Kromme.

Forty-five minutes remained—an eternity or the blink of an eye. For the Netherlands, it was all too brief. The clock outran Michels's men; no trace of *totaalvoetbal*. West Germany handily secured the win and the cup. When Taylor blew the whistle, van Hanegem bolted into the locker room and wasn't seen again, neither at the podium nor at the evening banquet. The atmosphere had none of the prematch tension. There was mutual respect, and perhaps something more, best demonstrated when Germany's Breitner and Holland's Johnny Rep swapped jerseys. It was a sign of friendship and more importantly a slap in the face for FIFA, which had banned swapping shirts on the field. Van Hanegem? Gone, holed up in his hotel room, fighting back tears. He would never bring himself to congratulate the winners. He had had a mission, a debt owed to the family he'd lost in that long-ago bombing. And he'd failed at it.

Zijn we er toch ingetuind (They ambushed us again). Those words, spoken by commentator Herman Kuiphof, are seared into the memory of every Dutch person that watched the drama unfold on July 7, 1974. Delivered at Taylor's final whistle, the phrase inextricably tied the Munich match to the events of the war: Germany versus the Netherlands to the Nazi invasion in 1940. In both cases, the Germans exploited the element of surprise. That's what Kuiphof meant. And most of his countrymen agreed. But it's worth remembering that Dutch soccer is an aesthetic. The 1974 defeat convinced part of the public that playing beautifully was even more important than winning. Cruyff put it best: "People stop me in the street and instead of complaining about the loss, they thank me for the football we played in that World Cup." That's one school of thought. The other believes that the Lost Final—capital letters intended—was the greatest trauma of the twentieth century, eclipsed only by the Second World War and the devastating floods of 1953. It's all a matter of perspective.

What is certain is that the 1974 final became an unintended bridge between generations. The youth, who'd only heard tales of the war from their parents, felt firsthand a sting reminiscent of that long-ago era, though not at the same scale. Now they too had been "ambushed" by the Germans—though this time there were no casualties, thankfully. There would be other matches between the Netherlands and West Germany, most memorably the 1988 European Championship semifinal on German soil. Of the players from 1974, Michels and Beckenbauer were still standing, the latter now a coach. Where Cruyff once fell short, Marco van Basten and Ruud Gullit succeeded. In Hamburg, the Germans took the lead from the penalty spot, only for the Dutch to answer in kind. It was just like that day in Munich, only the roles were reversed. Then, at the end of the game, Milan's striker delivered a brilliant move to seal a 2–1 victory. Van Basten had stepped into the shoes of Müller from fourteen years before.

Apparently nine million Dutch citizens—60 percent of the population—spilled into the streets to celebrate the victory. Many hoisted bicycles in the air. In every corner of the country the cry went up, "We've got them back!"—a pointed reference to the bicycles seized by the Germans when they entered Dutch territory in 1940. As Simon Kuper reports in *Football Against the Enemy*, the next day Jongbloed, the goalkeeper of the Dutch team defeated in Munich, sent a telegram on behalf of his old teammates to his soccer-playing grandchildren: "We have been delivered from our pain."

Whether he checked with van Hanegem before writing is anyone's guess.

POSTSCRIPT

As mentioned before, Wim van Hanegem was close friends with Wim Jansen, a midfielder for Feyenoord and the national team. In the summer of 1975, the two Wims and their wives were vacationing on an island in Zeeland. Van Hanegem had just received an offer from France's Marseille. He stood to earn a lot more there than at Feyenoord—ten times as much, according to some sources. But he had doubts. At some point he turned to Jansen and their wives and said, "Let's put it to a vote. Who's in favor of going?" The result? Two for, two against. Van Hanegem had a dog that never left his side. He looked him in the eye and said, "If you want us to go to Marseille, bark." The dog kept silent, thereby joining the nays. The family would remain in Rotterdam.

Is the story true? There are many alternative versions. Some say it happened before 1975, others claim that it was van Hanegem's daughters, not Jansen and his wife. But it's such a good story, why go digging into the past to find out? After all, the story captures the essence of van Hanegem's character. He was a man of principle whose deep, personal wounds never fully healed.

BFC

CHAPTER 10

A SUSPICIOUS DEATH:
THE COLD WAR, THE BERLIN WALL, AND A DIVIDED GERMANY

MATCH
Kaiserslautern vs. Dynamo Berlin

FINAL SCORE
4–1

WHEN
March 20, 1979

WHERE
Betzenberg Stadion, Kaiserslautern

MARCH 6, 1983. A Sunday. In West Germany, voters are heading to the polls for a snap election. The Berlin Wall still divides the city in two and will stand for another six years. Both the USSR and the United States have stationed Euromissiles—medium-range missiles with nuclear warheads—on European soil. Against this backdrop, as the whole world is watching, there is a pervasive sense of insecurity and instability.

Early elections are a rarity in Germany. Unlike in Italy, where governments and legislatures sprout and shrivel like mushrooms, Germany had only experienced such an event once, in 1972. Those most eagerly looking on are the "other" Germans, the ones in the East, where a new and unfamiliar restlessness has taken hold. Italian journalist Piero Benetazzo, writing for *La Repubblica*, captures the scene: "What we are witnessing in the GDR is the birth of a peace movement fueled by Western slogans and rhetoric. [Leader of the German Democratic Republic Erich] Honecker seems to have lost his magic grip on power. For the first time, dissent, once considered a phenomenon unique to the West, where conflict prevails, is beginning to emerge. By pointing out the regime's doublespeak and equivocations, the public is being given a tangible alternative view of things."

The East is watching, the West is voting. The victors are a coalition of Helmut Kohl's Christian Democrats and Franz Josef Strauss's Bavarian Christian Socialists—by a landslide. More shocking than the 48.8 percent share of the vote is the ten-point lead they hold over the Social Democrats, a margin surpassing even that of 1957, when Konrad Adenauer won an outright majority. In *Corriere della Sera*, Pietro Sormani offered this analysis: "Faced with the uncertainty posed by the Social Democrats' suggested equidistance between the two blocs, Germans have opted for the certainty of NATO membership, even if that means installing new nuclear missiles. Sunday's results made their preference crystal clear."

As a rule, Lutz Eigendorf didn't go to the polls. He had never shown an interest in politics. He was a professional soccer player, with other things on his mind. And he had spent the first twenty-three years of his life in East Berlin, where elections, as we know them in the West, didn't exist. A single party called the shots. Four years earlier, Eigendorf broke with his past and fled to the West, turning his back on the regime of Honecker, the much feared—especially by his fellow countrymen—head of the German Democratic Republic.

But there is a special reason why Eigendorf did not vote in the March 6 election: the young man lay in a coma in the ICU at Braunschweig. The night before, at 11:08 p.m., his Alfa Romeo had careened off the road near a curve and slammed into a tree. "Severe head and chest injuries," read the medical report. By 9:15 a.m. on Monday, March 7, his heart stopped forever. Based on evidence collected by the police and sent to prosecutors, the player was intoxicated at the time of the accident, with a blood alcohol level of 2.2 percent, equivalent to drinking four-and-a-half liters of beer or two liters of wine. There was no need for further inquiry. There was no autopsy performed, no examination of the wreckage.

Eigendorf, the investigators implied, had been asking for trouble.

"THE BECKENBAUER OF the East" wasn't a bad handle. Lutz Eigendorf had earned it for his poise on the pitch, for his upright bearing, and his orchestration of play. He was a baby when he joined Dynamo Berlin but quickly established himself as a leader.

They say he was the protégé of Erich Mielke, not exactly a nobody in East Germany. The powerful head of the Stasi,

Mielke could argue with Honecker, even contradict him, without fear of being sent off to shuffle papers in an anonymous office for the rest of his days.

The official title, Ministerium für Staatssicherheit, is a string of vowels and consonants easy to get tripped up by, especially if you're not familiar with the German tongue. Better to use the shortened version, the Stasi, which everyone can pronounce. The Stasi was synonymous with the secret police, surveillance headquarters, a laboratory suited for criminal practices—a structure to be feared, particularly if you weren't aligned with the powers that be. Dynamo Berlin was the club affiliated with the Ministry for State Security, and Mielke was a passionate soccer fan—a fanatic, according to those close to him. Players enjoyed special privileges, at least by the average living standards in the area, but Mielke demanded a lot from them, on and off the field. Above all, he insisted on their loyalty.

On Monday, March 19, 1979, sixteen Dynamo players, the coaching staff, and a significant number of agents boarded their bus bound for Kaiserslautern, West Germany. A friendly against the local team was scheduled for the next day: the top club in capitalist Bundesliga would square off against the top club in Communist Oberliga. On the night of their departure, Eigendorf and his teammates were required to sign a code of conduct agreement with the telling header "Distance from the Class Enemy." They were, in short, forbidden from any contact with Westerners. If anyone asked uncomfortable questions, players were to keep their mouths shut and report immediately to their managers. The friendly drew a modest crowd of 11,600 spectators. It was no contest: Kaiserslautern won 4–1. Mielke, promptly informed, couldn't have been pleased.

It would be Eigendorf's last time donning a Dynamo jersey. Late in the evening, the Beckenbauer of the East left his room, evaded the Stasi security, and made his way to the hotel bar. There he found Rudi Merk, the referee coordinator for Kaiserslautern and father of Markus Merk, who at the dawn of the new millennium would establish himself as one of the best referees in the world (he was entrusted with the all-Italian Champions League final in 2003, between Milan and Juventus, among many other prestigious matches). Eigendorf confided to him that he wanted to stay in the West. "Think carefully" was all the reply he got. It wasn't for nothing; the player had a wife and a two-year-old daughter waiting for him in East Berlin. As they said goodbye, Merk handed the player a business card. You never know when you might need it.

Dynamo's players got up early on March 21. They departed for East Berlin at 6:15 a.m. They had a scheduled stop in Giessen, in the Hesse region. At a large shopping center, they were allowed to spend what little Western currency they had received before leaving. The shopping spree lasted a full hour, then everyone got back on the bus. Everyone, that is, except Lutz Eigendorf.

"He must have had an accident," said one teammate. "He got lost in the crowd," said another. "Maybe he dozed off on a bench." They were all wrong. The star midfielder had simply gotten into a taxi and headed for Kaiserslautern. He handed the driver the business card he had been given the night before, with the word *Pariserstrasse* written on it. It was Rudi Merk's address. "Here I am," he announced when he arrived, as if to say, "I told you we'd meet again." Merk paid the driver the 375 marks for the fare and took Eigendorf to the office of Norbert Thines, Kaiserslautern's general manager.

Thus, Dynamo set off for East Berlin without its star player. Both the delegation head and the assistant coach stayed back in Giessen. The order from above was to wait for a representative from the GDR embassy in Bonn to determine if conditions were right for bringing the "deserter" back into line. Back in Kaiserslautern, they were facing an unprecedented situation: first they had to shield Eigendorf from the press and, more importantly, from retaliation by East German agents. The plan was to find him a temporary place to stay under a false name.

But the young man was terrified. He was afraid that he'd be kidnapped, killed even. Because he was unwilling to be left alone, Thines decided to have him stay at his place. He let him sleep in his bed, as if they were husband and wife or father and son. On the other side of the Iron Curtain, Mielke was furious. Defecting was the ultimate affront from his "godson" Eigendorf. He had to respond one way or another. After all, the Stasi existed precisely to deal with crises of this kind.

What happened in the four years that followed would largely come to light after the fall of the Berlin Wall, when the secret police archives were opened and files on tens of thousands of people could be accessed. However, if the fog of 1979 began to lift, it was partly thanks to the research of two people. Andreas Holy, a university student, was so struck by Eigendorf's story that he chose to dedicate his thesis to it. He said he examined 3,600 documents: a thousand from the police and the Braunschweig public prosecutor's office, and the rest from the Ministry of State Security. The other sleuth was broadcast journalist Heribert Schwan of *Westdeutsche Rundfunk*. Schwan would examine even more documents, somewhere in the range of tens of thousands. In 2000, he directed a documentary that would later become a book. Its title alone is chilling: *Tod dem Verräter!* (Death to the Traitor!).

Back to March 1979. The Stasi leapt into action as soon as news of Eigendorf's flight began to circulate. The bus carrying FC Dynamo had not yet arrived in East Berlin when two agents knocked at 3 Zechliner Strasse and asked Eigendorf's wife, Gabriele, to accompany them to a nearby police station. There was only one problem: who would look after little Sandy in her mother's absence? They had to find a policewoman to babysit the girl, which slowed the process down. It was after midnight when Gabriele was whisked off and interrogated for seven hours. The Stasi hoped to find out whether she was aware of her husband's plans and—here was what they really wanted to know—whether she intended to join him. The news knocked her sideways. She denied having any involvement and was eventually allowed to return home. But she didn't find her daughter there. The female agent had taken her somewhere, in part because the apartment had had to be cleared out so that bugs and other contraptions could be installed. Their correspondence was also monitored. It was business as usual for the Stasi. Not until after three horrifying days did Gabriele see her daughter again, and no one ever told her where she had been taken.

From that moment on, the secret police moved on three fronts: Kaiserslautern, East Berlin, and Brandenburg, where Eigendorf's parents lived. In the final tally, it turns out that roughly fifty people were involved in the spy operation, including working agents and so-called unofficial collaborators (informally known as IM, for Inoffizielle Mitarbeiter). That is precisely what piqued Schwan's interest: "My primary goal was to highlight how an extraordinary number of spies, in both the West and the East, were put on the trail of a single person and his closest affiliates, and how much money was invested for this purpose."

ONCE THE FEAR of the first few days had subsided, Lutz Eigendorf quickly grew accustomed to his new reality. He didn't even have a change of clothes with him, but that wasn't a problem. The president of Kaiserslautern, Juergen "Atze" Friedrich, owned a boutique and provided him with a new wardrobe. The Beckenbauer of the East was given a post at the club headquarters, a job more for show than anything else. At the same time, he coached the youth club—that *was* a real job. He performed it so well that the team racked up one victory after another and rapidly climbed the league ranks.

For Eigendorf it was just another way to pass the year of disqualification that FIFA regularly imposed in cases like his. Meanwhile, he was discovering the most intriguing aspects of life in the West. He bought a car only to trade it in shortly afterward, fell under the spell of the latest electronic gadgets, played tennis, and changed romantic partners as blithely as if he were changing clothes. His wife Gabriele wrote him just one letter, in early April. She reproaches him for his many betrayals, for instance, "when [she] was six months pregnant and [he] left on vacation with another woman." She tells him that Sandy keeps crying, asking when Daddy is coming home. But Eigendorf had no intention of returning. The former Dynamo Berlin star had only one thing on his mind: getting back out on the pitch. We can't say for sure if he knew that the prosecutor's office in East Berlin had issued a warrant for his arrest for violating Articles 100 and 213 of the Penal Code, those pertaining to the illegal abandonment of the country.

The plan that the Stasi contrived had elements of the diabolical: to plant a new love interest in the life of the still married Mrs. Eigendorf. Abandoned by her husband, she would need someone, the plan went, to provide her with a sense of stability and warmth. And here he was, Peter Hommann, the son of a driver for the Ministry of Security—a Stasi man. He knew Gabriele; they had dated in their youth. Obviously, Hommann was a spy in the pay of Mielke. He turned up with a bouquet of flowers, and she opened the door to her home. Espionage and techniques of seduction. The two married and had a child. Frau Eigendorf obtained a divorce and began the process of changing her daughter's last name: from then on she would be called Sandy Hommann. For her adoptive father, keeping apprised of things and regularly reporting back to his superiors is a cinch. (They could never be sure if the woman might be planning her own escape.) Mother and daughter only learn the truth about Hommann after the fall of the Berlin Wall and the opening of the Stasi archives.

The date Lutz Eigendorf had circled on the calendar was April 11, 1980, the day of the Bundesliga debut. Kaiserslautern was hosting Bochum and won handily, 4–1. The man who abandoned the East played the last twenty-four minutes, during which his club scored three of its four goals. The judgment of the newspapers and sports magazines were largely positive. Among the twenty-six thousand spectators in the stands was the spy Heinz Kühn, code name "Buchholz." He was a Stasi agent tasked with keeping a close eye on Eigendorf and reporting anything and everything about him: the make of his car, what and where he ate, how and with whom he spent his free time, the exact route he took from home to the training pitch, where he parked, even whether he locked his car door when he arrived at the facility. On the evening of their victory over Bochum, the Beckenbauer of the East went to the Big Ben nightclub—in good company, naturally. Agent Kühn/

Buchholz made a note of everything, even the brand of champagne he ordered to celebrate his debut.

The coach at Kaiserslautern was Karl-Heinz Feldkamp, one of the most highly regarded coaches in Germany. He liked Eigendorf and played him in various positions, once even as a center forward. But as the weeks went by, the young man who fled from the East was no longer playing at the same level he was when he arrived. His physical condition had deteriorated noticeably as a result of his lifestyle off the pitch, which left a lot to be desired. During that time, the Stasi decided to replace the spy initially assigned to Eigendorf. Kühn was over sixty and perhaps no longer as reliable as he had once been, so his place was taken by the younger Karl-Heinz Felgner, code-named "Schlosser," a former GDR boxing champion whom Eigendorf had met when he was playing at Dynamo. Felgner had no trouble rekindling their friendship; the player even invited him into his home from time to time.

It's one of the Stasi's "victories." Another was the plot in Berlin. Gabriele and Hommann were getting along swimmingly. The two go on vacation, take a car with a driver—a colleague of his father, essentially—and stay at a hotel provided by the Ministry of Security. Records from that time include the following: "Upon returning from vacation and under pressure from our mole, Gabriele threw most of the personal belongings of the traitor Eigendorf into the trash." Which is essentially what happened at Dynamo Berlin; Eigendorf souvenirs, official photos, and a thousand glasses engraved with the deserter's name were disposed of.

Besides tennis, Lutz Eigendorf threw himself into other pastimes, some he probably didn't even know existed when he was at Dynamo. Waterskiing, for one. During the 1980–81 season winter break, he turned up in Israel, where he had an accident that kept him off the playing field for several weeks. The Stasi took note and added it to his file. But there was more. Eigendorf loved flying and at one point got it into his head to earn his pilot's license. Not only were the lessons expensive, they clashed with his soccer schedule. But that didn't bother the playboy, and one fine day he asked to be excused from soccer training. Karl-Heinz Feldkamp's jaw dropped. Never in his coaching career had he heard such a request. "At first," he'd later recount, "I thought he was joking. [Eigendorf] was already someone who frequently changed houses and cars. Technically, I had noticed things about him that were off. When he asked about the flying lesson, I realized he was losing control of his life."

Eigendorf and Kaiserslautern were destined to go their separate ways. In the summer of 1982, the soccer player moved to Eintracht Braunschweig, where he signed a two-year contract for 180,000 marks per season. He got what he wanted: to stay in the Bundesliga, secure a spot with a prestigious club, and earn a lot of money. His new coach, Uli Maslo, was counting on him: "We knew everything about him: that he was one of the best players from the GDR, that he had started strong at Kaiserslautern but then ran into problems. We had a lot of young players on the team and his experience could be useful to us." It didn't change much for the Stasi: the squad assigned to monitor Eigendorf simply had to pack their bags and move 250 miles north.

In the reports that found their way to Mielke's desk in East Berlin, the name Josephine began cropping up more often. She was a high school student who had stormed into the player's life. This time, the relationship seemed serious. During her high school graduation trip, Josi (as she was known) traveled with her class to Berlin and while there took the opportunity to meet her boyfriend's parents. With a child already on the way, the pair married on October 25, 1982. Their son would be born early in the new year.

"Keep an eye on Eigendorf," Mielke commanded his closest associates, again and again. The man he confided in most often was Heinz Hess, lieutenant colonel in the Stasi and head of the Central Coordinating Group, an organization created to curb defections to the West. The phenomenon had already stricken soccer in the GDR. A few weeks before Eigendorf's defection, Jörg Berger, who managed the GDR's Under-21 team, had fled. In total, around a hundred top athletes had turned their backs on East Berlin. In 1979, on the thirtieth anniversary of the Democratic Republic, the magazine *Bunte* ran an article addressed to the GDR: "Ihre Besten sind im Westen" (Your best are in the West).

Eigendorf's foray at Eintracht Braunschweig got off to the rockiest start imaginable. During preseason, the player injured his Achilles tendon and was forced to miss the first thirteen games. He made his debut on November 20, in Stuttgart. It was the same old Eigendorf: now and then he'd put in a good performance, and sometimes he'd even play outstanding soccer. But inevitably he hit a wall.

Monday, February 21, 1983, was a crucial date. In the early evening, the regional TV station, Sender Freies Berlin, broadcast a long interview with the player. It was not the first interview Eigendorf had given, but this one was special, if only because of the location. They were broadcasting from Berlin, right in front of the Wall, mere feet from the Dynamo stadium where Eigendorf had made his name. The interviewer asked him about GDR soccer and why a country that dominated sports like swimming and athletics failed to excel in soccer. "It's because too much attention is paid to the collective and too little to the individual," said Eigendorf. "Talented players don't have the freedom they need to express that talent." Then came the jab: "If there is no opportunity for individuals to develop and fulfil their potential in the private sector, how could you expect there to be on a soccer field?" To say that his comments didn't sit well with Mielke is a gross understatement. Though we'll never know for sure whether those words jump-started a "final solution" for the player, it is quite plausible.

On February 27, Eigendorf was on the field when Eintracht Braunschweig lost to Borussia Dortmund. He played poorly, and the yellow team scored one of its goals thanks to his having lost the ball. The next match was scheduled for March 5, against Bochum. The Beckenbauer of the East sat on the bench for the entire ninety minutes, despite his team losing 2–0. The mood was grim. He was consoled by President Hans Jäcker, who came up to him at the end and said, “I’ve spoken to the coach, you’ll be in the starting lineup next time. After all, you can’t play any worse than that.” But there would be no next time for Lutz Eigendorf.

Holy and Schwan have retraced the evening of March 5 minute by minute. First, Eigendorf joined some of his teammates at the team’s favorite restaurant, where he ate and drank one or two six-ounce beers. Then he went home to watch the highlights of the afternoon’s game before getting back in his car. He had an appointment with Manfred Müller, his flight instructor. They met at a bar near the airport. Eigendorf booked his first medium-haul flight, destination Sylt, for the following day. He drank another small beer, two at most. Müller would reiterate this with absolute certainty in the documentary about the incident. The two men bid one another farewell at about 10:00 p.m. An hour or so passed before the accident. An hour that is shrouded in mystery.

How much had Eigendorf had to drink before leaving the bar? According to Schwan’s reconstruction of events, which was corroborated by witnesses, between three and four six-ounce beers, not nearly enough to explain a blood alcohol level of 2.2, a level that, as we mentioned at the beginning of the chapter, means consuming four-and-a-half liters of beer or two liters of wine. The most extreme theory is that as he got into his car the player was kidnapped, forced at gunpoint to drink a mixture of alcohol and poison, and told to disappear. Terrified and confused, he drove as far as the curve where the accident occurred. There, a car coming in the opposite direction flashed its headlights, causing him to lose control of the vehicle. And then he crashed into the tree. There is no concrete evidence to prove this, only clues. A handwritten note was found in the Stasi file on Eigendorf, with words and phrases highlighted, including "stun," "accident statistics," "rendered powerless from outside," "anesthetic." And the most important of all: "Eigendorf."

After a disturbing detail came to light, Schwan wondered if it wasn't the former boxer Felgner who was assigned the mission. In the Stasi archives relating to the movements of Eigendorf's "friend," all documents between 1980 and 1983 are missing. A coincidence? Maybe. But one thing is certain: on the day of the player's death, Felgner received a bonus of five hundred marks from the Stasi. Lieutenant Colonel Heinz Hess was paid one thousand marks for his "extraordinary service."

Hess died in 2004, four years after being summoned by the Berlin police for questioning, but he had been careful not to show up. No further action was taken. As for Felgner, he reappeared in the news in 2011 when he was arrested for theft in a grocery store in Düsseldorf. During the trial, he issued a statement that went something like "I should have killed Eigendorf, but in the end I backed out." It was a surprising admission, a real head-scratcher, especially considering that the court was investigating a completely different matter. For the record, Felgner had an alibi for the evening of March 5, 1983. There remain, and at this point will remain forever, many gray areas—from the failure to perform an autopsy on Eigendorf's body to missing documents and absent witnesses.

Everyone's entitled to their own opinion.

There's one last piece to conclude this dramatic story. On Monday, March 7, 1983, Dynamo Berlin was on its way to Stuttgart for a friendly, not unlike the one they played in Kaiserslautern in 1979. This time, the team did not stop at a shopping center and the players' every movement was closely monitored. There would be no repeat of the Eigendorf case, not ever again. As they got off the bus, the team heard the news. Eigendorf had died from injuries sustained in an accident two days earlier. It was an eerie coincidence. If any of the players had even remotely entertained the idea of staying in the West, Eigendorf's tragic end gave them more than enough reason to refrain from acting on it.

CHAPTER 11

KICK IN THE TEETH: THE COLLAPSE OF YUGOSLAVIA AND THE WAR IN THE BALKANS

MATCH
Dinamo Zagreb vs. Red Star Belgrade

FINAL SCORE
Match terminated due to rioting

WHEN
May 13, 1990

WHERE:
Maksimir Stadium, Zagreb

FOR SOCCER FANS, 2024 was all about the European Championship. It was a tournament that, if you scanned the record books, the finals, the roll call of winners, essentially added up to a World Cup minus Brazil, Argentina, and Uruguay. In other words, it was the best of the best, with only the above exceptions missing. But there was one national team that didn't play in the Euros—because it no longer exists, though it did exist four decades ago. A country so brimming with soccer talent that the thought of what it might look like today is enough to send a chill down your spine. Picture this lineup:

Jan Oblak in goal.

A back line featuring Joško Gvardiol, Stefan Savić, and Amir Rrahmani.

In midfield, Ivan Perišić, Luka Modrić, Sergej Milinković-Savić, and Eljif Elmas, with the attacking midfielder Dušan Tadić just ahead of them.

And leading the line, Edin Džeko and Dušan Vlahović.

Three Serbs, three Croats, one Slovenian, one Montenegrin, one Kosovar, one Macedonian, and one Bosnian. And ready to come off the bench are the likes of Marcelo Brozović and Miralem Pjanić. Suffice it to say the squad would have been serious contenders for the European crown.

But now they're scattered across various national teams because, at a certain point, history took a different course. Had they only been born forty years earlier, these eleven players would have been teammates. They would have donned their blue Yugoslavian jerseys, sung the Yugoslavian anthem, and shaken hands with Yugoslavian dignitaries. They'd have been the pride of a soccer tradition that, since the Second World War, has generated talent and garnered applause everywhere it goes.

Applause more than trophies. On various occasions, the crown had slipped their grasp just moments before the final whistle. Take the 1968 European Championship. They were playing against Italy, in Rome. Yugoslavia was ahead 1–0 and about to expand their lead, only for Angelo Domenghini to hoof it into the net ten minutes from time. Yugoslavia would lose two days later in the replay. "That's the Slavs for you: brilliant to watch but lacking in finish. They're incurable individualists, anarchists, madmen"—that has been a common refrain in private notebooks or with the microphones switched off. They were dubbed the "Brazilians of Europe." Hyperbole? That depends. It's no coincidence that Belgrade's main stadium is called the Marakana, a nod to Brazil's Maracaña. And if that weren't enough, in 1971, Pelé himself chose to play his last match for Brazil against Yugoslavia.

YUGOSLAVIA WAS MADE up of six republics and two autonomous provinces. Of various ethnic groups, various religions, various languages, and various alphabets. For nearly thirty years, from 1953 until his death in 1980, the glue that held the country together was Josip Broz Tito, leader of the Non-Aligned Movement, meaning aligned neither with the United States nor with the Soviet Union. After the Second World War, Tito recognized that sports in general, and soccer in particular, were fundamental to the Socialist Federal Republic.

The marshal's death on May 4, 1980, stripped Yugoslavia's socialist project of its legitimacy, plunging the nation into a political crisis that would simmer for years and eventually boil over into war—a crisis born, in part, from the passing of this charismatic figure who had somehow hidden the absence of a true national identity.

The day Tito died was a Sunday, a day, even in Yugoslavia, reserved for soccer. According to journalist and author Gigi Riva's beautiful book *L'ultimo rigore di Faruk* (Faruk's Last

Penalty), the news came while Hajduk Split was playing Red Star Belgrade, Croats versus Serbs. Hajduk captain Zlatko Vujovic broke down in tears. His teammates and opponents did likewise. People were crying in the stands, too, and then there rose a song in tribute to the leader: "We will never stray from your path." Little did they know, they would not keep their promise.

After Tito's exit, a collective body was established, made up of eight members, one for each republic and autonomous province, with a rotating presidency. It would do little to stem the tide of mounting problems. Economically, the decision to embark on the road of self-management did enormous damage. The debt to international monetary institutions rose to well over $20 million; unemployment soared to 25 percent of the working population, sometimes double that among Albanians in Kosovo. Not to mention inflation, which was running at around 100 percent in 1980 and skyrocketed to 2,000 percent by the end of the next decade. Yugoslavia was like a car with no driver, careening toward its doom.

There will come a time when chilling terms like *ethnic cleansing* and *genocide* will become common parlance. There will commence the kind of war that leaves tens of thousands of innocent victims on the battlefield. Europe will turn back the clock by some forty years, to an era when bombs rained down across the continent. For my Italian compatriots, this time people will be dying fifty minutes away—the time it takes for NATO planes to fly from the Italian Air Force base in Falconara to Sarajevo.

Weapons will be used first in Slovenia—for a few days and with limited bloodshed—and then in Croatia. These are the first two republics to break ties with Yugoslavia. They are also the ones with the highest quality of life, the ones that have always been closest to Western Europe. Ideological differences aside, they are fed up with paying taxes to settle the deficits of the other republics.

MAKSIMIR STADIUM IS the largest stadium in Zagreb and the one with the richest history. To this day it is where Croatia's national team plays its most important matches. The name Maksimir means "maximum peace." At the entrance, in the northern stands where networks of fans gather, is a memorial with the following inscription: TO ALL DINAMO ZAGREB FANS, FOR WHOM THE WAR BEGAN IN THIS STADIUM ON MAY 13, 1990, AND WHO SACRIFICED THEIR LIVES ON THE ALTAR OF THEIR HOMELAND.

On that day Dinamo Zagreb faced off against Red Star Belgrade. It was Croats against Serbs, the Balkans's version of Barcelona vs. Real Madrid. It's a valid comparison; during the Franco years, Barcelona's Camp Nou stadium was one of the few safe harbors where people could express dissent without risking immediate arrest. Only, in what was still called Yugoslavia, things were taken to another level, with machine guns replacing innocuous chants and fans dressing up as soldiers ready to do anything, even kill.

Dinamo is a source of pride for Zagreb, so much so that under Tito it was allowed to retain the Croatian checkerboard in its crest. On the Sunday before the big match, Croatia held its first free elections, a further step toward the dismantling of Yugoslavia. The winner was the HDZ party, or Hrvatska Demokratska Zajednica, the Croatian Democratic Union. Its leader was Franjo Tuđman, a man who had lived many lives. A Communist partisan during the Second World War, he accompanied Marshal Tito's rise to power, supported him in everything he did, and eventually became responsible for training the Yugoslavian army's cadres. Later, Tuđman became a staunch nationalist, departing from the political positions of his youth. He was expelled from the party and wound up in prison on charges of anti-Yugoslavian activities. In short, he became the symbol of aspirations for Croatian independence.

As far as soccer was concerned, the match between Dinamo Zagreb and Red Star wasn't all that important. The Belgrade team was already the Yugoslavian champion for the seventeenth time, and their opponents had to settle for second place. In a report published two days after the match in the *Corriere della Sera*, Eros Bicic wrote: "According to predictions, the Red Star–Dinamo derby may as well have been a friendly. Preparations had followed normal procedure. Management had requested ninety-one police officers to handle roughly twenty-five thousand ticket buyers." Ninety-one police officers, one per 270 fans. Under normal circumstances, that might have been fine, but there was nothing normal about what was about to take place. Three thousand fans left Belgrade, almost all of them members of the Delije

(Serbian for "heroes"), the most extreme Red Star ultras. Their undisputed leader was Željko Ražnatović, alias Arkan ("The Tiger"). Arkan had been convicted multiple times for a disturbing combination of murders, armed robberies, and prison escapes. It's easy to imagine how he managed to organize various factions of hooligans and transform them from loose cannons into a disciplined army. Arkan and his followers would show their worst side during the siege of Vukovar in the summer and fall of 1991 and later in Bosnia, which cost the lives of thousands of innocent Muslims.

The Delije's railway journey from Belgrade to Zagreb would "train" them for what would happen a few hours later at the stadium: wrecked carriages, shattered windows, terrified passengers. Bicic's report in *Corriere* continues: "Small groups of Red Star supporters arrived in Zagreb, some on Saturday evening, others during the night and on Sunday morning. The first acts of hooliganism took place on the streets of the Croatian capital: bystanders were beaten, cars were damaged, shop windows were smashed. One clash cost a policeman his eye. By just 10:00 a.m., over fifty people had been arrested, while fans of Red Star had been escorted to the south stand of the stadium."

Dinamo Zagreb's fans were equally prepared to do anything. They called themselves—in English—the Bad Blue Boys, BBB for short, a name reminiscent of the gangs of young Americans in the 1983 film *Bad Boys*, starring Sean Penn. Most of them, writes Simon Kuper in *Football Against the Enemy*, came from the suburbs of Zagreb, "so depressing that it is a shock that certain blocks of flats are still standing." The Bad Blue Boys were founded in 1986, and they have been recruiting followers in and outside the city ever since. What defined them? A lot of sympathy for Franjo Tuđman's political party, for one. They had heard that the Delije had come from Belgrade and wanted to be ready.

It wouldn't be like other matches. In the end, it wouldn't be a match. Soccer was just a pretext for the encounter; in the eyes of many, what was clear was that sheer hatred had transformed one's opponents into one's enemies, who had to be destroyed at all costs. They were mostly young men who, when war broke out, would not hesitate to put on a uniform and go fight their adversaries. Not all of them would return.

THE MOOD IN the streets of Zagreb was tense, in stark contrast to the clear sky of what felt like an early summer day. But the worst was yet to come—the stage was set at Maksimir Stadium. The chants didn't bode well: "Zagreb is Serbia! We'll kill Tuđman!" shouted Red Star's fans. "When you're happy, knock a Serb on the ground, gut him with a knife, and shout, 'Independent Croatia!'" responded the Bad Blue Boys.

The teams walked onto the field to warm up, and every object you can imagine started flying from the stands. The opening salvo came from the Delije side. They ripped up plastic seats and advertising boards and hurled them onto the pitch, all while the announcer was still reading out the lineups.

That this vandalism was premeditated can be proved by the fact that fans from both sides had come armed with acid to eat through the metal barriers separating the stands from the pitch. Then everyone was on the field, seeking out the "enemy." All hell broke loose. The players—teammates and opponents alike—exchanged bewildered looks. Many of them played for the national team and, a few days later, would come together to take on Italy in the World Cup. Realizing they couldn't just stand there, most of them put their athleticism to work and sprinted for the locker rooms.

Then there was the matter of law enforcement. In 1990, just under 15 percent of the population of Croatia was Serbian. Many found work in the army and police. And on the day of the match, those officers on duty at the stadium swore allegiance to their ethnic affiliation, brutally targeting Dinamo Zagreb fans while ignoring the other side, as if the Croatians alone were to blame for what was unfolding.

A HANDFUL OF players remained on the field, and that handful was in Dinamo blue. One of them hadn't turned twenty-two yet, but already he was the youngest captain in the club's history. His name was Zvonimir Boban, and he was considered one of the brightest prospects in Europe. He sported No. 10—in soccer, the number of legends. Italy was in his future, but on that day all that mattered to him was Dinamo Zagreb.

At the end of his career, Boban described one of his defining qualities as the ability to "think on his feet." That skill came in handy during the maelstrom at Maksimir. Looking right and left, he saw the police had made their choice, chasing after the home supporters. When one officer attacked a young fan, the Dinamo captain snapped: he charged forward and performed a flying kick, kneeing the officer in the face. The whole thing was caught on camera by Zagreb television.

The image was captured and consigned to the annals of history. Had it happened during play, it would have been a red card for life, no need for VAR. The officer was left prostrate with a broken jaw, but before capitulating he had time to trade insults with Boban. Members of the Bad Blue Boys rushed to their captain and escorted him to the locker room, the safest place at that moment. Every night for the next twenty days Boban slept at a different friend's house, for fear of retribution or arrest.

Needless to say, Dinamo vs. Red Star wasn't played. But that didn't prevent CNN from ranking it among the five soccer matches that changed the world. The final toll: 138 injuries—59 fans, 79 police officers—and 132 arrests. There were other incidents, too: trams vandalized, cars reduced to scrap. At least no one was killed. If you were dying for a bit of good news that day, that was it. The rest was heartbreak.

ZVONIMIR BOBAN IS a thinking man's player. His horizon doesn't end at the playing field, nor does he repeat commonplaces like "play every game like it's your last" or "respect your opponent, don't fear them." He earned a degree in history from the University of Zagreb with a thesis titled "Christianity in the Roman Empire." He has never been afraid to speak his mind, and his management career has been a natural extension of his playing career, only in suit and tie. Sometime later, he spoke about that day in May at Maksimir for Vuk Janic's documentary *The Last Yugoslavian Football Team*:

> May 13 is a very important date in my life. On that day I entered political history, not just the history of the sport. It started when the rioters from Belgrade began demolishing our stadium. The Zagreb police, who were pro-regime, let them, as if it were normal. But, for our Dinamo fans, it was not normal. Then the police took sides. They started beating up our fans. I cursed at the police and one of them hit me. I reacted by hitting him back. He fell. In the days that followed, I grew twenty years older. At that time and under that regime, it was like committing suicide. I was afraid something bad would happen to me. But my reaction was human. From a Christian point of view, I made a mistake. But the policeman hit me first. Jesus says to turn the other cheek if someone slaps you. But he didn't say what to do when you get slapped on both cheeks.

Many saw Boban's flying kick of the policeman as a symbol of rebellion. Some went so far as to regard it as the spark that set off the Balkan Wars—like the shots fired by Gavrilo Princip in Sarajevo on June 28, 1914, which killed Archduke Franz Ferdinand, heir to the Austrian throne, and triggered the First World War. But the Serbian nationalist student was advocating for the unification of all South Slavs, and in 1990 Yugoslavia was breaking up.

More than thirty years later, Zvonimir Boban prefers not to revisit the subject. What needed to be said has been said. However, of one thing he remains convinced: kicking the policeman in the face was "an act of rebellion against a regime that had never before shown such dishonesty toward the Croatian side." Boban goes on to say that he was just one of many young people in Zagreb demanding democracy and freedom and that, though the match was linked in some way to the war, it did not trigger the war, which did not erupt for another year. The situation may well have deteriorated without the clash at Maksimir Stadium because, according to Boban, the regime did not want to follow the path of democracy or accept the idea of a Yugoslavian confederation. Boban would do it all over again. He does not regret a thing. Not one thing.

Over the years, various historians have studied the possible connections between the Dinamo Zagreb–Red Star match and the outbreak of the Balkan Wars. I contacted Professor Dario Brentin, a researcher at the University of Graz who has written numerous articles about the subject. In his opinion,

The riots of May 13 were just the tip of the spear, played up by the media yet effective for radicalizing organized groups of supporters that had already been involved in similar incidents in previous years. In this particular case, we have to start from the assumption that there was a disproportionate number of ethnic Serbs in the police and army. The perception was that the national security apparatus was largely responsible for maintaining Serbian dominance within federal Yugoslavia. That contributed to the incident at Maksimir Stadium. There were also two other important factors that set it apart: it was covered on live television and fell just weeks after the first free elections in Croatia, which were won by parties in favor of Croatian independence. Meaning it was a very politically charged moment. In reality it would be a mistake to think that the match sparked the war. Later, toward the end of the 1990s, it would accrue significance for the story Croatia told about the collapse of Yugoslavia. That and nothing more. Although I can't offer any proof, I am convinced that war would have broken out anyway. What is clear is that Boban's violent act guaranteed him a place in the pantheon of Croatian folk heroes. One other thing. It's ironic that, given all that desire to turn people into symbols, the policeman whom the player struck

> wasn't Serbian. Refik Ahmetović was a Bosnian Muslim from Tuzla. But in that moment he was seen as a symbol of Serbian nationalism.

Zvonimir Boban was banned for six months, preventing him from participating in the 1990 World Cup. At the time, Yugoslavia was coached by Ivica Osim, who was born and raised in Sarajevo, the most multiethnic of the major Yugoslavian cities. Osim is a sage of soccer who, as Gigi Riva writes, embodies "the impossible hope that, at least for the month of the competition, brotherhood and unity, the two key words on which Yugoslavian socialism was based, will have meaning." The players somehow managed to get behind him, if only out of respect for his person.

BUT THERE THE equanimity ends. A friendly against the Netherlands, their last before flying to Italy, was scheduled for June 3. Where? In Zagreb, at Maksimir Stadium. It could hardly have been called a bright idea to play just twenty days after the events that got Boban disqualified. The crowd booed the Yugoslavian anthem, chanted offensive songs, and threw its support behind the other team for the entire match. The Dutch wound up winning 2–0. "We didn't know there were so many Dutch fans around here," kidded Ruud Gullit and Marco van Basten. Everyone came in for criticism, Osim especially. He was accused of snubbing the Croatians on the team. The first to add fuel to the fire were journalists, for whom the coach had never masked his contempt. "The press," he said one day, "has always criticized me. Everyone wanted players from their own republic on the national team, but I always went my own way. I didn't care where they came from. All that mattered to me was whether they could play. The best players always played. I'd have played eleven Albanians from Kosovo if I thought it was the right decision."

Any and everything has been said or written about Ivica Osim. Some claim he once drank eleven bottles of whisky in a single night. He always defended himself with wit and irony, even responding in French to questions from Yugoslavian journalists. He prepared for the World Cup as if he were coaching the national team of a united country, where everyone was rowing in the same direction. But Yugoslavia was slowly imploding, headed for a disaster that no one could yet imagine.

Amid all this, Yugoslavia reached the quarterfinals. It did so despite a run marked by wild swings: they played terribly in the opener against West Germany, tepidly against Colombia, convincingly against the United Arab Emirates, exceptionally in the round of sixteen against Spain. The next obstacle was Argentina, the reigning world champions, led by Diego Armando Maradona and ten other players. The match of a lifetime was set for Saturday, June 30, in Florence. In the pages of *Corriere della Sera*, journalist Roberto Perrone trained his sights on Osim: "His plan was to arrive at this moment by walking on a bed of nails that his players and the thousand ethnic groups they belong to set under his feet every day. He succeeded, enduring the jeers and insults from the very first day, when he didn't let a single Croatian play in Zagreb. Osim is the Richard Strauss of coaches: gifted with imagination. And he must possess a large imagination given his firm belief in a team of small but great wonders who have the attitude and feet of a Platini but far less follow-through on the field."

In hindsight, Yugoslavia could have won that World Cup. Instead, they were knocked out in the quarterfinals by Argentina, on penalties. Forced to play with ten men after the thirty-first minute, when Šabanadžović, Maradona's defender, was sent off. Yet they created the game's best chances to score. When the match went to penalties, Osim withdrew to the locker room; for him, the game ended at 0–0. Safet Susic, the most charismatic player, gave the referee the list of players who would take the penalty kick. The fifth man up was Faruk Hadžibegić, a Bosnian Muslim who would have gladly sat this one out, after having missed from the spot against Colombia, but evidently there were no other "volunteers." They needed a goal to even the score and continue the penalty shoot-out, but Faruk's shot rolled gently into the arms of Argentina's Mauro Goicoechea. That was the end of the World Cup, the end of the dream, the end of everything. Or almost. While Yugoslavia, with all its republics and provinces, was relentlessly spiraling toward war, the national soccer team continued to play—and win. It qualified for the 1992 Euros in Sweden, topping its group ahead of Denmark.

Given the circumstances, it was nearly a soccer miracle. But the tale doesn't have a happy ending. On May 23, less than a month before the opening whistle of the tournament, Ivica Osim resigned. He threw in the towel, citing "solidarity with my Sarajevo, destroyed by a pointless war." What he did not mention publicly were the death threats hanging over him and his team.

Somehow Yugoslavia still made it to Sweden, but it did not play in the Euros, having been expelled from the tournament just days before kickoff. The UEFA did not want to host a national team whose country was at war. Denmark—its players scattered on summer holiday—was hastily brought in to replace them. And it would go on to win the tournament, writing what became a fairy tale for everyone. Everyone except those who were expelled from the Euros right before they took the field. The question lingers: How would Yugoslavia have fared? I am referring, of course, to the "real" Yugoslavia and all its best players: Dragan Stojković, Zvonimir Boban, Robert Prosinecki, Dejan Savicević, Siniša Mihajlović. The same question dogs us to this day. How far would a national team with Modrić, Milinković-Savić, Perišić, and Džeko get today? Here's a clue: Croatia—a remnant of that "old" Yugoslavia—finished second and third in the 2018 and 2022 World Cups.

EPILOGUE

PARIS'S LONG NIGHT: EUROPE AND TERRORISM IN THE NEW MILLENIUM

MATCH
France vs. Germany

FINAL SCORE
2–0

WHEN
November 13, 2015

WHERE
Stade de France, Paris

THREE MEN, TERRORISTS, enter the field disguised as security. England has just taken the lead against Tunisia with a goal by Alan Shearer, and Takeshi Okada is about to signal for halftime. One of the fake guards runs toward David Seaman in goal. He's got on a belt packed with explosives and blows himself to pieces, taking with him Seaman and several photographers stationed behind the goal. The second terrorist approaches England's bench. He's got two hand grenades. He throws one at Beckham and his teammates, and the other into the crowd. It's carnage. There's one kamikaze standing and his mission is to shoot Shearer. He carries out his orders diligently and, before being killed by a police officer, points his gun at Teddy Sheringham and Paul Scholes. In twenty seconds, half of England's team is dead. Osama bin Laden has sent his message to the world.

THIS IS THE account of an event that fortunately never occurred. Nobody died in Marseille on June 15, 1998, and England and Tunisia's qualifier for the World Cup proceeded as scheduled, with England coming out on top 2–0. But it could have been otherwise. Al-Qaeda had, in fact, hatched an intricate terrorist plot that would have been broadcast across the globe, an act meant to unfold just as I've told it but was foiled weeks earlier thanks to the intelligence work of the principal countries in Europe. Bin Laden's biographer, Adam Robinson, reconstructed the story in minute detail in his 1992 book *Terror on the Pitch*. Robinson envisaged what the apocalyptic scenario would have looked like had the terrorists carried out their plan. He even imagined a post-match press conference in which FIFA's new president, Sepp Blatter, announced the end of the World Cup.

The idea was to end this book, a blend of soccer and history, with the events that led up to the Balkan War. Eleven chapters, eleven matches. Eleven, same as the number of players on a team. But more than thirty years have passed, and a lot has happened in the interim. It's too wide a gap to ignore. Before and after the end of what Eric Hobsbawm called the short twentieth century, history has continued to cross paths with that ball rolling forward and twenty-two young men in shorts chasing after it. And it has done so with increasing intensity and frequency. There are dozens of matches to choose from. But you inevitably have to make a selection, starting, perhaps, with one word: terrorism.

I begin with England versus Tunisia because, in a certain sense, it represents a watershed moment, capturing a dramatic development in the relationship between soccer and violence. True, nothing happened in Marseille on June 15, 1998, but that was only because in the weeks leading up to it, French intelligence agencies, in collaboration with other countries, including Italy, identified and dismantled the cell entrusted with sowing chaos at the stadium.

The men belonged to the Algerian-based Groupe Islamique Armé. They were supplied forged credentials and security uniforms to wear when entering the Vélodrome. But they never showed up at the stadium, having been neutralized just in time by counterterrorism officers. The massacre would have been unprecedented, a horror show served up for half a billion viewers worldwide. Something that could have altered the way we see soccer as a mass phenomenon and drawn a line between a "before" and an "after."

The attack had been planned down to the last detail. The stadium in Marseille was just one of the targets; at the same time, a second commando unit was supposed to storm the Paris hotel where the US team was staying. With the team crowded around the TV to catch England and Tunisia, it would likely have been another massacre. And then came the most disturbing part: someone was to hijack a commercial airliner and crash it into the Civaux nuclear power plant, within spitting distance of Poitiers, in the heart of France. It was a test run for September 11.

June 15, 1998, should have gone down in history as one of the darkest days on record. Fortunately, things turned out differently. Police forces in France, Belgium, Italy, Germany, and Switzerland stopped just shy of a hundred terrorists who meant to carry out simultaneous attacks. The plan was orchestrated by Osama bin Laden, the leader of Al-Qaeda, whose many criminal plans included physically wiping out the best of British soccer. This was the same man who, in his years studying in London, had shown more than a passing interest in Arsenal, even attending several of the Gunners' home games.

BUT LET'S SKIP ahead to November 13, 2015. Bin Laden had been dead for four years. The world had somehow put the trauma of September 11 behind it, despite having to reckon with terrorist attacks in Madrid, London, and other major cities. A new radical Islamist organization, Daesh—known in our part of the world as ISIS, short for the Islamic State of Iraq and Syria—had taken control of large parts of Iraq and rallied new militias on an international scale. The West was under attack from Islamic jihad, with its calls for holy war in the name of Allah, but it was trying to act as if nothing was happening, to chase away the ghosts, to return to normal life.

There were seven months to go until the European Championship, which, just like the 1998 World Cup, would be hosted by France. Because Didier Deschamps's team was hosting, it automatically qualified and only played friendly matches. That November day, Germany was up. It was a rematch of the 2014 World Cup quarterfinal in Brazil, when the Germans eked out a victory and went on to win the title.

In 2015 Islamic terrorism had already exacted a heavy toll in France. An attack on the Paris office of the satirical weekly *Charlie Hebdo* that January had claimed the lives of twelve people. Ten months later, life appeared to have returned to normal, though tensions remained high. November 13 began with two bomb threats in the capital: one at the Gare de Lyon and the other at the Hotel Molitor on the Left Bank, where the German team was staying. These were not the first such threats, and they wouldn't be the last. At the time, Oliver Bierhoff was the manager of Die Mannschaft, and I asked him about what happened that day: "I was in a meeting with other federation officials when I got a phone call. They told me there was a bomb threat and that we had to evacuate the hotel. I assembled the team in the lobby and we left. We didn't have to wait long, just enough for the police to make sure everything was fine. It was clearly a false alarm, nothing to worry about. Now and then someone picks up the phone and makes threats that are, perhaps, the product of a sick mind."

After lunch, a short break, and a pre-match meeting, everyone boarded the bus to the Stade de France. Same drill for the French, who were staying at Clairefontaine, France's national football center thirty miles outside the capital. Such preparations are the standard before every match. That evening, eighty thousand people crammed into the stadium, plus three members of a jihadist commando unit intent on carrying out a massacre. It's possible that the attackers, extremely young and coming from neighboring Belgium, ran into heavy traffic and arrived late, which may have upset their plans. Each wore an explosives-packed suicide belt, fully aware that their lives would end in the seconds it took to press a detonator. What mattered to them was that they weren't the only ones to die.

It isn't clear whether the three men had tickets. The first of the three approached the turnstiles at gate D and tried to force his way past security. A guard became suspicious, prompting the attacker to flee along Avenue Jules Rimet, the street bordering the stadium. At 9:20 p.m., he blew himself up near one of the bars where fans had gathered. A sixty-three-year-old Portuguese man who had the misfortune of being in the wrong place at the wrong time, Luis Dias, was killed in the blast. Had the bomber managed to enter the stands or blend into the crowd, how many more might have died? At the time of the explosion, France's Patrice Evra had possession of the ball. The fullback paused, confused. He glanced around, then went back to playing the game as if nothing had happened. Over the next half hour, there were two more explosions, both outside the stadium, and two more attackers blown to pieces. Bierhoff later searched his memory for details of that night:

> The explosions were quite loud. Nothing like the kind you sometimes hear in stadiums. When that happens, the crowd usually reacts with disapproval. That didn't happen, it was met with pure silence. I was in the stands. France's President Hollande was sitting a few feet away from me. I suddenly saw a commotion around him. It was a group of security guards who helped him up and whisked him away. That was when I realized something serious must have happened, though I couldn't imagine what. Maybe it was an isolated incident, a lone actor; a large-scale terrorist attack planned by several people was inconceivable. Then word began to spread that there had been shootings in central Paris. But it wasn't clear whether they were connected to what had happened outside the stadium.

Paris, and all of France, had practically stumbled into a war. ISIS's men had chosen to launch an attack on a Friday evening, when restaurants and cafés were packed. They cried out "*Allahu Akbar*" before striking indiscriminately, for no other reason than to avenge French airstrikes in Syria. Their number one target was the Bataclan theater, where California's Eagles of Death Metal was playing a show. In prior years, the Bataclan had received threats from Islamic organizations after hosting evenings organized by Jewish or pro-Israeli associations, but no one had ever thought of taking special security measures, not even after the attack on the offices of *Charlie Hebdo*, located a few hundred meters from the theater. "In the last ten months," wrote Anais Ginori in *La Repubblica*, "Paris has lulled itself into thinking that the January attacks were just a bad dream, when in fact they were a dress rehearsal for raising the bar of horror even higher."

In the Bataclan alone, the death toll eventually rose to eighty-nine, not counting the terrorists who blew themselves up when security forces stormed the theater. Meanwhile, the game went on at the Stade de France. During halftime, the two coaches, Didier Deschamps and Joachim Löw, were briefed on what was happening. The picture that emerged was, by necessity, partial, not least because the worst was yet to come in the city. The two teams were asked to finish the match: the least bad option, at that moment. The public began to realize that Paris was under attack; after all, all you needed was a smartphone to get real-time updates.

Leaf through a soccer annual or do a quick search on the internet, and you'll see that France won the match 2–0, with goals from Olivier Giroud and André-Pierre Gignac. But that is the least important fact. As the minutes ticked by, the match lost all meaning. Almost ten years later, the question remains relevant: Was it right to continue playing? "Say it wasn't a mistake," explains Bierhoff.

> At that point in time, the reports coming in were hazy and no one knew exactly what was happening.

> In the climate of uncertainty and fear that had been created, the stadium was still a safe space. From my point of view, it was important to bring order to the flood of information that was overwhelming us, to get an idea of the situation and to establish who was ultimately responsible for making the decision. Looking back, I can say that I'm proud of how I handled that moment. The president and vice president of our federation were also there, but they kept their distance. In the end, I took charge of the situation, while remaining, obviously, in close contact with the police and security personnel, both French and German.

As a first precaution, all the exits were closed, at least temporarily. The crowd remained in the stadium. Some in the stands, some on the pitch. Almost without realizing it, couples and parents with children found themselves treading the grass where, seventeen years earlier, Zidane, Thuram, and their teammates had hoisted the World Cup in the air. It could have been a thrilling moment, but of course at the time no one thought to connect the present moment with past glory. When the crowd was finally allowed to leave the stadium, they spontaneously broke into the "Marseillaise." It sent shivers down your spine.

Meanwhile, France and Germany sought refuge in their respective locker rooms. "The reasoning," continued Bierhoff, was simple. As long as we stayed locked in there, no one could threaten us. Every half hour I took stock of the situation and informed the players and staff of the latest developments. It was important no wild and unfounded rumors spread, nothing picked up on some dubious website. Should we stay or go? At that point, no one could say whether there would be more attacks or where they would be. We knew that people were being shot and killed in the city, that was all. At a certain point, it was nighttime, the police suggested we return to our hotel, guaranteeing us maximum protection. They told us not to worry, that they would station their men around the building to prevent anyone from even approaching. Our security chief said to me, "Oliver, you saw what happened at the stadium and what's happening in the city. If you ask me, they'll never be able to guarantee our safety." He was right. Then we thought about it some more, starting with the bomb threat that morning. Maybe it wasn't just some crazy guy acting alone, maybe it was all part of a plan to target us. At that precise moment in history, Germany was in a position of political strength. The terrorists' aim may well have been to strike a highly symbolic target such as the German national soccer team. Kind of like September 11 with the United States and the Twin Towers. We had to be very careful.

> There was no going back to the hotel. The goal was to leave Paris immediately once we left the stadium. Obviously, we needed a plane to take us back to Germany. In the drama of the moment, we got lucky, because the CEO of Lufthansa was attending the match and came down to the locker room with us. He assured us that a plane would be made available to take us from Paris at seven in the morning. At that point it was clear to everyone that we would not leave the stadium except to go to the airport.

They spent the whole night shut inside a locker room, eating sandwiches and stretching out on makeshift beds, attempting, in vain, to rest. It was a far cry from the routine that athletes of that caliber are accustomed to, all the comforts they enjoy in their daily lives. I asked Bierhoff if he remembered anything in particular about those hours. "Honestly," he said,

> no. I do remember that the players never lost their cool. They spent the time talking to each other or playing games. Not once did they panic. I had a kind of direct line to Chancellor Merkel, with whom I had an excellent relationship. I called her as soon as I sensed the gravity of the situation. A staff member of the federation expected her to send in the army to escort us home. But it wasn't like Merkel could do all that much from Berlin. She told me, "You're free to do what you think best under

> the circumstances." That gave me confidence. After a while, things went back to normal. It didn't even feel as though we were part of such a dramatic event.

Then the team returned home. At dawn, on a grief-stricken Saturday, the Germans left behind a city brought to its knees, mourning its 130 dead. Lassana Diarra, a member of the French team, lost his cousin. His teammate Antoine Griezmann's sister had been at the Bataclan and was saved by a miracle. Among the victims there was also a young Italian woman, Valeria Solesin, a sociology student from Venice who had also been attending the concert at the Bataclan but was not as fortunate as Maud Griezmann. Bierhoff continued: "Once the emotion of the moment had subsided, I began to think about what might have happened had even one of the attackers blown himself up inside the stadium, in the middle of the crowd. Those thoughts stayed with me during the three days leading up to our next match against the Netherlands."

That's right. Because in the relentless churn of the soccer calendar, there are only a few windows reserved for national teams, and the most must be made of them, cramming two matches into four days. Germany had to get back out on the field in Hanover for another friendly, this time against the Netherlands. You can imagine the mood. In a sane world, the match would have been called off, but not in Berlin's corridors of power. It was decided that Angela Merkel and half the federal government would be in the stands because Germany–Netherlands had to become a showcase for freedom. "Their presence was to be symbolic," wrote Danilo Taino in the *Corriere della Sera*, "to show that life goes on despite ISIS and to express solidarity with France and Paris."

On the bus carrying Germany to the stadium in Hanover, Oliver Bierhoff's thoughts raced.

> I imagined crazy scenarios. I thought about the threat that drones might pose. What if one of them had dropped a bomb on the field or in the stands? You're a prisoner to fear. You realize that when you're the target of an enemy you can't see, you'll never be safe twenty-four hours a day. Meanwhile, the bus was moving. We were twenty minutes from the stadium when my cell phone rang. It was Federal Vice President [Reinhard] Rauball. His exact words were: "Tell the driver to stop the bus immediately, turn around, and go back to the hotel." When someone in that position gives you an order like that, you immediately think that if you don't turn around and keep going, there's a bomb just ahead, ready to detonate the moment you drive by.

The report came from foreign intelligence, likely French, and spoke of credible plans for a bomb attack on the stadium. Other sources suggested the entire city of Hanover could be under threat from an Islamic attack. Playing was out of the question. Thousands had already taken their seats and were ushered to the exits. Just as in Paris four days earlier, the crowd filed out without betraying the slightest sign of panic. Meanwhile rumors swirled. Some said there'd been an ambulance packed with explosives, others that a lone spectator had been stopped while trying to enter the stadium with a suspicious package. "The risk to Germany and Europe is high," said German Interior Minister Thomas de Maizière. Unlike the France-Germany match, we'll never know if an attack in Hanover was truly imminent. What's clear is that a threat, however unfounded, was enough to set the entire security apparatus in motion.

While Germany versus Netherlands was canceled, another friendly went ahead as scheduled, a classic European showdown between England and France. There were no bomb threats at Wembley. The most poignant moment came before kickoff, when both teams gathered at midfield to sing the "Marseillaise." The players lined up shoulder to shoulder, one Frenchman for every Englishman, rather than splitting into their usual squads. The crowd joined in, a gesture far from guaranteed given the rivalry between the two nations, which extends well beyond soccer. The anthem's lyrics were displayed on the stadium's jumbotrons: eighty thousand spectators sang as one, Prince William and Prime Minister David Cameron among them. "This time," wrote Fabio Cavalera in the *Corriere*, "as never before, and all rhetoric set aside, the love of soccer transformed into political solidarity against terrorism. The caliphates want to sow fear and destroy our pastimes, soccer included. So Wembley stood firm against the forces of religious hatred, and the friendly between England and France became a symbolic pact. London is Paris, Londoners Parisians."

Soccer versus terrorism. It sounds like the headline for a soccer match. Except in this case, human lives are on the line. Sometimes things turns out well; sometimes they end in tragedy. Take Brussels, for instance. On October 16, 2023, Belgium was hosting Sweden in a Euro qualifier. To the now sadly familiar cry of "Allahu Akbar," an Islamic fundamentalist shot and killed two people in the city center. Both were wearing Swedish jerseys and were on their way to the stadium. The news broke while the teams were already on the field. At halftime, the Swedes approached Italian referee Maurizio Mariani and asked him to suspend the match. They were in shock and simply couldn't go on. A familiar scenario unfolded: spectators were trapped inside the stadium for hours, subway stations were shut down, and residents urged to stay home. Meanwhile, the attacker posted a message on Facebook claiming responsibility and describing himself as a "soldier of the Islamic State." He wouldn't live much longer. The next morning, the police tracked him down in a bar. He was still armed with the machine gun that he'd used to kill the two fans. He tried to flee, but the officers shot and killed him. Belgium and Sweden were supposed to play another half, but no one wanted to. After the first forty-five minutes of play, the match was called at 1–1.

On that day, terrorism won. But luckily that hasn't always

been the case. Across the century we have traveled in this book, soccer has proved time and again that its power to unite people is inexhaustible. It has united them in times of war and in times of peace, in the wealthiest corners of the planet and in the poorest. The simple act of chasing a ball has aroused emotions, forged destinies, and changed the course of history, even off the field. Yes, today the flow of money and thirst for power have shuffled the decks. Teams have turned into brands, as have players—at least the most famous. Fans are no longer fans but customers. Yet the feeling you get watching a dribble, an overhead kick, or a backheel remains undiminished. And that makes you think that soccer is still a fundamental part of our lives, that it still has the capacity to make our hearts beat faster.

ACKNOWLEDGMENTS

There are many people I'd like to thank for helping me identify and select the material used to write this book. My thanks also go to those who, in various capacities, were directly involved in the matches recounted in these chapters, particularly Joe Jordan, Zvonimir Boban, and Oliver Bierhoff, whom I asked to rewind the tape, sometimes by as much as half a century.

Roberto Beccantini, a close friend since our longstanding collaboration at *La Gazzetta dello Sport*, took it upon himself to reread this book from first sentence to last and excise the inaccuracies that inevitably cropped up. I am deeply grateful to him for his invaluable contribution. For more specific assistance, I am grateful to Giampaolo Muliari, director of the Museo del Grande Torino, who provided me with an abundance of documentary evidence about that wonderful team. My Viennese colleague Bernd Fisa helped me reconstruct the figure of Matthias Sindelar and shed light on the role of Austrian referee Erich Linemayr in the Chile–Soviet Union affair. Likewise, Michael Novak was a wellspring of information on Lutz Eigendorf, whom he had known and befriended during his years as a journalist, while Filippo Maria

Ricci, with his boundless knowledge of African soccer, was key to painting a picture of Zaire in 1974. The journalist and former Ajax manager, David Endt, is an institution in the Netherlands; calling on him to comment on van Hanegem and related matters was a no-brainer. My thanks to him, too. Outside the world of soccer, I should mention Professor Dario Brentin, with whom I spoke about the connections between the 1990 Dinamo Zagreb–Red Star match and the Balkan Wars.

In closing, I'd be remiss not to mention the support of the Bolzano Civic Library, its director Ermanno Filippi, and his colleagues, first and foremost Matteo Meloni. It was there that the book began to take shape. All this—and here we come full circle—was guided by Lorenzo Costantini, my editor at Il Saggiatore, who, despite being miles away, never failed to make me feel he was close by.